KNITTING YARNS
and
SPINNING TALES

A KNITTER'S STASH OF WIT AND WISDOM

EDITED BY KARI CORNELL

VOYAGEUR PRESS

First published in 2005 by Voyageur Press, an imprint of MBI Publishing Company, Galtier Plaza, Suite 200, 380 Jackson Street, St. Paul, MN 55101-3885 USA

Edited by Kari Cornell
Designed by Maria Friedrich
Cover art: top photo © Solveig Hisdal, from her book *Poetry in Stitches*; bottom photo © David P. Austin.

Printed in China

Library of Congress Cataloging-in-Publication Data

Knitting yarns and spinning tales : a knitter's stash of wit and wisdom / edited by Kari Cornell.
   p. cm.
  ISBN-13 978-0-89658-725-0
  ISBN-10 0-89658-725-8
 1. Knitting—Fiction. 2. Knitters (Persons)—Fiction. 3. Short stories, American. 4. Knitters (Persons) 5. Knitting. I. Cornell, Kari A.
  PS648.K55K58 2005
  746.43'2—dc22

                       2005007342

CONTENTS

Chapter 3:

WORLDLY KNITS

Chapter 4:

TO BE A KNITTER

Chapter 5:

THE ZEN OF KNITTING

Chapter 6:

GETTING HOOKED ON CROCHET, KNITTING'S SECOND-COUSIN

INTRODUCTION

Shortly after I was born, my mother taught herself to knit from a book, making herself a beautiful gray sweater with a complicated cable pattern. Unfortunately, the sweater was too small, and so, after it languished in the bottom of a dresser drawer for a year or more, she finally packed it in a paper grocery bag with a few other discarded items of clothing and toted it off to Goodwill.

I don't think I would have heard the story of the sweater had I myself not learned to knit, some thirty years later. When my mother first told me about it, I was shocked that she had given the sweater away. The very idea brought to mind a flood of questions. Did the sweater still exist? Where was the sweater now and who had worn it over the years? And, perhaps most importantly, could I have worn it at some point? How many more sweaters would there have been had mom continued to knit?

A year ago last Thanksgiving, I taught my mother to knit . . . again. The two of us toured local yarn shops one overcast Friday afternoon in search of the perfect project, needles, and yarn for her to begin. We found a simple but fun scarf pattern that called for a funky variegated yarn to be knit lengthwise on a circular needle. She selected a couple of skeins in shades of blue, green, and gray, and we headed home. She boiled water for wild raspberry tea before we sat down in the living room where I taught her how to cast on and then showed her the knit stitch.

The going was awkward at first, but by Sunday evening she had completed her first scarf, dropping only a few stitches along the way. I was impressed with her progress. Over the months that followed, she knit several scarves, each one better than the last. She's since expanded her repertoire, knitting a sweater ("It looks store-bought!" my husband exclaimed) for herself and an adorable cap and sweater set for my son Will.

For each of us, knitting has become more than a craft to occupy our time during long car rides or while watching TV in the evenings. Knitting has become something my mom and I share. These days, when we talk on the phone each week, we ask each other about our knitting projects.

- - - -

We exchange ideas, give each other knitting books as gifts, and work through rough spots together.

In a way, our knitting relationship is a microcosm for the larger knitting community. No, I can't physically gather with knitters from around the country to knit and chat as I do with my mom or members of my knitting club. But I can collect the essays of knitters from all over North America into this book for knitters everywhere to read, relate to, and share with others.

The essays in this collection range from shearing sheep on a Sunday afternoon in March to an evening in Sant'Arsenio, Italy, where women gather on their doorsteps to knit, crochet, embroider, and chat. Other essays delve into the psyche of the knitter—What is it that makes us want to collect skein after skein of yarn that we may never use? Why do we find those romantic scenes depicted in pattern books so entrancing? Why is it that the appetite for new knitting projects always seems so much greater than what we can actually achieve in a lifetime?—and, because crochet has become increasingly popular among knitters over the past few years, you'll find a few essays by those who've become hooked on crochet. I hope you enjoy them all.

Chapter 1

ALL IN THE FAMILY

"ONE OF MY EARLIEST MEMORIES HAS ALWAYS BEEN OF A DAY WHEN I PESTERED MY MOTHER TO TEACH ME HOW TO KNIT."

—*Elizabeth Zimmermann,* Knitting Around, *1989*

The survival of a craft such as knitting often rests on the shoulders of elders, who graciously pass the skill down to the next generation. The teacher usually is someone in the family—a grandparent, parent, aunt, or uncle. Although the story of learning to knit is a universal one, the essays in this chapter reveal that the beginning knitter walks away with more than just knitting know-how. Many times they also gain a greater understanding and appreciation for the person teaching the lesson.

KNITTING DAUGHTER

BY PERRI KLASS

Memory works in mysterious ways. Years ago, writer Perri Klass taught her daughter to knit, hoping to pass on a favorite pastime. In her essay "Knitting Daughter," which first appeared in the Spring 2004 issue of *Knitter's* magazine, Perri interviews her daughter about the experience and discovers that her daughter remembers many details about the lesson that Perri herself had long forgotten.

Perri Klass is a pediatrician in Boston, and medical director of the national center for Reach Out and Read. She is the author of several books, including *The Mystery of Breathing* and *Love and Modern Medicine*. Klass is a regular columnist for *Knitter's* magazine. A collection of her columns, *Two Sweaters for My Father,* was published by XRX in 2004.

My daughter Josephine is in tenth grade, and she hasn't touched her knitting in years and years. And of course I have my comedy routines about life with a teenage daughter (the eye-rolling . . . the moods . . . the making me feel I'm the stupidest person in the universe . . .), and presumably she has her comedy routines about life with mother. And I wanted to write about teaching her to knit, but I wanted to write about it honestly—without too much saccharine nostalgia for the child she was, not so long ago, without too much false and self-congratulatory enhancement of my own skills as a mother, and above all, without pretending that the lesson really "took." You mothers of adolescent daughters, I think, will understand that treacherously easy nostalgia for the lost cozy days of uncomplicated hugs, and most will probably also understand the mild trepidation with which I proposed to her, finally, a formal interview.

Do you remember learning to knit?

"I think it was around third grade when you taught me to knit. You would alternate nights when you would teach me to knit and nights when you would read to me, and then when I got good enough you would read and I would knit. I think you were reading Frances Hodgson Burnett's *A Little Princess* and *The Secret Garden*."

(Oh, my God, I had completely forgotten that. I had remembered teaching her to knit, but I had forgotten that it was linked to reading aloud, and certainly to any special books. But the minute she said it, I thought of the beautifully illustrated editions of those two books that I read aloud to her—the wonderful Graham Rust illustrations—and how I wouldn't let her see the movie of *A Little Princess* when it came out until we had finished the book. And I was suffused with a warm glow that was partly nostalgia and partly a sense that hey, guess what, I really was a pretty good mother, wasn't I?)

How did I teach you?

"That little rhyme—under the fence, catch the sheep, back we come, off we leap. That's basically how I would remember how to do it today. You guided my hands—you always cast on for me, and you were always catching my dropped stitches."

(And I had forgotten the rhyme. In fact, I began to wonder exactly what memories I was cherishing when I originally thought back on teaching Josephine to knit, since I seemed to have retained no details whatsoever. It made me wonder how many other basic details of my children's growing-up have completely escaped me—how many pro-

- - - -

found and essential colors and sounds and sensations that must once have seemed precious, unforgettable, and completely characteristic, are now forever out of reach. Yes, there are the details after which I yearn—that precise smell of the silken baby head, remembered with love but never to be recaptured—but how many moments are so unrecognizably lost that I don't even know they're gone? I didn't know whether to get all weepy for my own lost-memory moments, or for Josephine's superior recall—you parents of adolescents will probably understand the impulse that rose in me, instantly suppressed, to say to her, tremulously, "So you remember the feeling of me guiding your hands—and you remember it fondly?")

The first thing you knit?

"The first thing I knit was a purple and turquoise scarf, and I gave it to my grandmother. I picked the yarn. We used to go to the yarn store, and I liked looking through the yarn and their cards of buttons. I was always a really tight knitter and it didn't build fast enough, it took a very long time to make substantial progress, so you told me to loosen my stitches and then the first part of the scarf looked really tight and the later part looked loose and I was upset by that."

(Well, I'm a tight knitter myself, but I do remember that Josephine was unable to allow any slack on the yarn at all. Back and forth she went, with her needles, generating a tiny knot of a scarf, the yarn wearing too deep and sore a groove into the finger around which she had it wrapped. I supplied her with larger needles, and I reminded her every couple of rows to loosen up, and I think she tried. But you are what you are, and I'm not sure you can change your knitting tension any more than you can change your signature—I mean, you can pretend it's something different, something belonging to someone else, for a while, but you know what's really you.)

And then what?

"I knit a few things for my doll's house—I remember a pink striped blanket. But my next real project was that sweater. We looked through this book you got me, *Kids Knitting,* and I remember I liked the pattern because it reminded me of a red sweater I had at the time that I liked a lot, curled at the sleeves and neck. So I chose the pattern, and we went to the wool store and I looked at all the wools; I knew I wanted to make it striped, I was thinking pink and purple, and I ended up with fuchsia, purple, and bluish violet. I remember we spent some time looking for skeins from the same lot because you told me that they would be closer—the same dye batch. And I started with the back because you told me I was going to like the first part I did

- - - -

least—and sure enough, there were all these little blemishes, there'd be these really loose stitches and things would be a little uneven, I was always dropping stitches, it drove me a little crazy because as you know, I'm a little bit of a perfectionist."

(That sweater, now, I remember vividly. She worked on it and worked on it, and, well, it was never finished. That sweater was her knitting career, at once her great and showy success, with three colors and a complicated pattern, and a major garment growing in her third-grade hands, and also her disillusionment. It was that sweater that danced teasingly before my eyes when I wanted to write about teaching my daughter to knit, as if I had taught her not the skill or the joy, but instead all the habits I like least in myself, the overambitious grandiose yarn purchase, the fear of finishing, the bits and pieces left to languish somewhere in a bag.)

What did you like best about knitting?

"I loved picking out yarn and choosing colors and putting together colors. I liked the repetition of the hands, I liked that I could knit and listen to you read—it wasn't exactly multitasking, but it felt productive. And I enjoyed the productive feel of it, doing something with my hands. It made me less restless. Sitting listening to somebody talk or read—I notice it in classes, too; I like to draw or write or make little squiggly lines, I get a little restless when I'm not doing anything but just listening. I liked making things but again, it troubled my soul a little that it wasn't as neat as yours."

(I wanted to say, 'Oh, but how could it be as neat as mine, when I've been doing this for decades.' I wanted to say, 'Don't be so hard on yourself, you were getting better and better,' I remember that. I wanted to say, 'Don't be such a perfectionist in life that you can't let yourself learn something new.' And I also wanted to say, 'Oh, I know exactly what you mean about doing something with your hands when you're listening to someone talk. I've always felt that way, and it's part of why I knit, and part of why you should take it up again.' And I didn't say any of these things because I didn't want to break the bubble of the interview, didn't want to change her tone by reminding her of mothers and their tendency to draw moral lessons about life, or even by suggesting to her that we had too much in common.)

When did you stop? Why did you stop?

"I think it directly coincided with you guys not reading to me—maybe when I changed schools and had homework to do and I could read pretty much anything on my own.

– – – –

At a certain point, I put it away in that bag, constantly made resolutions, but I never did it. Maybe my life got busier. I don't like the idea of being defeated, it's very troubling. I've never gotten myself up to attack it again. I think I have a fear of finishing it and not liking it. I do think about it, I think I'd like to knit, but with the amount that the uneven stitching or the little mistakes I made troubled me—I really felt like I'll never wear this, I'm always going to be thinking about that loose stitch over there."

(I thought of apologizing—I'm so sorry I stopped reading to you, I hope to hell it was because your life got busier and not because mine did, and isn't it awful that neither of us can quite remember how it happened. I thought of offering whole new projects, new trips to the yarn store, colors to be chosen, practice swatches to be thrown away until her stitches are perfect and even, row after row. I thought of expounding one of those moral lessons about life with a reminder that the little flaws and irregularities of a hand-made item are to be cherished. Instead, I nodded a matter-of-fact interviewer's nod, and asked my last question: Can you find that sweater? And she jumped up and left the room, and came back in less than a minute with a bulging plastic bag, opening it up and laying out the pieces of her sweater, looking at them for the first time in more than six years.)

- - - -

"I still love the colors—I adore the colors—but here we have an example of what I mean—look at these huge stitches! Here are my front and my back—the front looks okay, the back is much bigger, more misshapen—here's one sleeve, I love the curl at the cuff—here's my other sleeve still on the needle—fifteen stripes on the finished one, thirteen on the one on the needles—it looks awfully loose, which is funny considering I started it six years ago! I still adore the way it curls—probably if I saw the finished sweater hanging in this style in a store I would like it, but it's all the little blemishes I know so well that make me agonize over it. It does look better than I remembered it—certainly I didn't remember how lovely the color scheme was."

(I watched her stroke the sweater, saw her marveling at her own work. Yes, she was identifying big loose stitches and other small irregularities, but she was also recognizing her own taste, her own skill, her own effort. However she had imagined this sweater—a childish botched project— she was seeing the colors that she herself had recognizably chosen, the lush bulky wool soft to the skin, the intriguingly rolled-up hem and cuffs. I know that feeling, when you look at a long-sidelined project and see again the beauty that originally drew you, and wonder, how could I have let this go after so much work? I took up the unfinished sleeve—abandoned in the middle of a purl row—and finished the row and then the stripe, as if I could somehow alleviate some of the uncertainty and dissatisfaction that had held this garment in suspended animation while Josephine herself grew from third grade to tenth. I could block this, I said. It wouldn't be so hard to finish. And it's so big it would still fit you, or you could give it to someone—you could give it to one of your grandmothers! The colors are beautiful and it's very warm and of course, I did allow myself to say didactically, all your little mistakes will just make it more beautiful. The interview was over and the businesslike interviewer was gone. Could Josephine tell that in fact I was suddenly trying to correct every complicated tension of adolescence, to bring back every lost sweet mother-daughter memory, to teach her every valuable lesson that might spare her pain later on? She smiled at me forbearingly as I worked on the almost-finished sleeve, and she said very kindly, though rather dubiously, "Well, maybe. We can always try and see how it comes out.")

– – – –

IN HONOR OF GRANDMA, BASEBALL, AND KNITTING

BY MICHAEL DREGNI

In this essay, author Michael Dregni recalls an experience many knitters share: learning to knit at his grandmother's knee. His story "Learning to Knit: A Romantic Tragedy in Four Acts" appeared in *For the Love of Knitting: A Celebration of the Knitter's Art.* He is also the editor of *Knitticisms and Other Purls of Wisdom.*

I don't know too many superheroes. Muscles of steel, X-ray eyes, skin-tight leotards that look suspiciously like pajamas, flowing capes, able to leap tall buildings, and halt speeding locomotives.

I don't know too many superheroes, but my grandma came close.

They just don't make grandmothers like they used to. My grandma was born in 1899 at the end of one century and the dawn of another. Her parents were immigrants from

Sweden who settled in the barrens of central Minnesota, on a farm quickly and wisely abandoned for the growing metropolis of Minneapolis. My grandma often reminded us that her childhood chores included milking the cows, kneading the daily bread until her muscles ached, and washing dishes by age five. These were common enough duties for the era, but seemed close to heroic to us grandchildren with store-bought milk and bread and a dishwashing machine that needed nothing more than the push of a button.

But these childhood chores were the least of it. What made us grandchildren marvel was the fact that Grandma could do *anything*. Catch the most fish at her lake cabin, then clean a walleye with just a few practiced swipes of a knife. Plant flowers that blossomed out of a garden of pure sand. Win at cards most every game, be counted on to shake a Yahtzee. Stoically do away with extra kittens with the blunt end of a catsup bottle. Pilot a speedboat, drive a car as big as a house, chop firewood with an evil-looking double-bladed axe. And then go inside and cook magnificent meals. Here was a little, old lady—curlers under her hairnet, apron around her waist—and we were all in awe.

Yet even this was just the beginning. Grandma wielded a needle like a wizard with a wand.

Most of us today have one hobby, maybe two. For my

grandmother, our so-called "hobbies" were necessities, and she was equally competent with knitting needles, an embroidery needle, a crochet hook, and a mending needle.

In the evening after us kids helped her with the dishes in the cabin kitchen, she settled into her rocking chair to watch her beloved Minnesota Twins baseball team on television and she pulled out her latest project. Whether it was darning a holey sock or repairing some clothing, the day's work was not yet over.

Most of this work furnished the house, harking back to the days when families made most of their own clothes and blankets. Grandma crocheted slippers for everyone in the family, then made a new pair when the old wore out. Still armed with her crochet hook, she made afghans in blazes of colors—acrylic yellows, lurid reds, tropical lime greens, and oranges better suited for hunting wear. Her afghans featured big patterns that no one could miss: foot-wide stripes and hallucinatory zigzags, multitudes of multihued granny squares, and even one afghan that was simply one huge granny square gone wild. The blankets were Grandma's little nod to luxury.

Turning to her knitting, she churned out scarves, hats, and sweaters to keep us warm. And to protect herself from the heat of the stove, heavy-duty potholders were made—although unwisely fashioned from acrylic yarns.

Beyond the necessities, Grandma also added beauty to everyday household items. Every sheet and pillowcase in her house was enlivened by an embroidered motif of songbirds or flower blooms. Flour-sack dishtowels bore bright needlework designs to cheer up a dreary thrice-a-day job. Curtains were fashioned from gingham and then edged with crocheted lace. The Christmas tree was festooned with knit and crocheted ornaments. Even all of her clothes hangers were beautified by multicolored crocheted coverings.

Grandma's needlework was always competent and always reliable—although her baseball team wasn't. She'd shut off the TV in disgust for days, boycotting "those damn Twins" when they weren't winning.

She also taught us grandchildren to work a needle, and while she had no time for a losing baseball team, she was patient in helping us kids. There were seven grandchildren—one girl and six boys—and at one time or another we all were under Grandma's tutelage.

I learned how to embroider while watching an afternoon ballgame one summer when I was about nine. Grandma cheered on her favorite, Tony Oliva, cursed

Harmon Killebrew for striking out again, then calmly directed me in embroidering a cowboy onto my own pillowcase. Knitting was a bit more complex, but soon I was making useless swatches like a pro. She also taught me to crochet, and I churned out yards—maybe even miles—of chain stitch for no real reason than to be like my grandma.

For my grandmother's generation, needlework was a necessity. It wasn't a hobby, although it was a pastime. It was also an opportunity to create; out of this necessity, needlework was a license to make art during the drudgery of daily life, whether that art was beautiful knitwear, stunning quilts, or the charm of an embroidered pillowcase.

For my mother's succeeding generation, needlework seemed to be a chore and nothing more; a feminist motto of the time warned that "Needlework is wasted womanpower." Sure, there were some great fiber artists, but by and large, people were more affluent and could buy what they needed instead of making it. Few bothered to darn or mend anymore; new clothing was cheap and easy. Knitting moved from being a necessity to becoming a hobby—and a hobby often associated with the older generation and with work. My mother sometimes knit and continued to teach us children, but she also had new interests and her knitting was usually set aside.

And now my generation comes along and picks up the knitting needles and crochet hooks again with enthusiasm. After days spent working with computers and other inhuman, disconnected tasks, we hunger for the creation of needlework. And many of today's knitters wholeheartedly embrace all of the stodgy, old-fashionedness as well as adding a new, modern flair.

Grandma would be pleased.

My grandparents died twenty-plus years ago now. Their house was sold and their belongings given to their children and grandchildren, as happens. Grandma didn't live to see the Minnesota Twins win the World Series. Twice.

Yet my grandparents' lake cabin, built by them in 1940, is still in the family and it seems no matter how many years go by that it will always be called "Grandma's cabin."

Inside, it's a museum. The knotty pine walls are hung with framed paint-by-numbers made by Grandma and the couch is covered with her afghans. Some of her embroidered pillowcases survive in the linen closet amidst the newer store-bought ones, partly melted acrylic potholders hang beside the range, and the closets still glow with her rainbow-colored, crochet-covered hangers.

And even now, I still stand in awe.

– – – –

CELLOPHANE BUTTERFLIES, PINOCHLE, AND BROWN ACRYLIC

BY GRETA CUNNINGHAM

In "Cellophane Butterflies, Pinochle, and Brown Acrylic," author Greta Cunningham writes fondly of both her grandmothers, but admits that neither taught her to knit. Instead, she acquired the skill from an unlikely source: a World War II veteran with an amazing ability to make use of brown acrylic yarn. Greta is a newscaster and program host on Minnesota Public Radio.

I'm from a family where the women have their noses in books and their fingers in a box of chocolates. Most knitters I know learned the craft from their grandmothers. They have tales of afternoons spent casting on and clacking away with patient grannies. My knitting friends bring out baby hats and christening gowns stitched by their grandmothers. I do not have such stories nor do I have any handmade baby garments.

My paternal grandmother, Peg, was Irish American and spent most of her life living in a row house in Queens, New York. She was a college-educated woman who loved Harlequin romance novels, reruns of *M*A*S*H,* and crossword puzzles. She always encouraged her grandchildren to do well in school and to find joy in life. For her, crafting was limited to taking the cellophane wrappers from two pieces of hard candy and twisting them into what she called "butterflies." As children, it took us a while to figure out she was making these "butterflies" as a ruse to avoid getting up from her comfortable reading chair to dispose of her wrappers.

My maternal grandmother, Flo, retired to a condo in Florida. She was Swedish American and sported flowered bathing caps as she sat by the pool perfecting her Pinochle game. Her life was spent waging a battle against dirt and grime. During my visits with her I recall never actually touching fabric—plastic covered her couch, chairs, lampshades, and carpeting. Her passion was cleanliness, and a bottle of Clorox Bleach was never far from her reach.

My two grandmothers taught me a lot about life but they did not teach me a thing about knitting.

I learned to knit from an unlikely source—a World War II veteran named Max. I don't recall exactly what prompted

- - - -

me to sign up for the community education class. But I know I was anxious to learn how two sticks and some string could make fabric. We were asked to show up for the first day of class with size 7 needles and a skein of acrylic yarn. The class was held in an old elementary school that was converted into an adult learning facility. A group of twelve women sat in desks that were too small for adult frames, and waited for the instructor.

Our teacher, Max, looked exactly like Jack Albertson—the actor who played the Man in *Chico and the Man* and Grandpa Joe in *Willy Wonka and the Chocolate Factory*. He entered the dimly lit classroom toting a projector and a large carousel of slides. He told us we would not actually touch our needles this first night of class. Instead, we would see a slide show of his knitted creations.

The first slide featured a knitted king-sized bedspread in brown acrylic yarn. Max told us it took him the better part of a summer to knit up the shiny-looking bedding. He clicked to the next slide and said, "My wife got tired of the brown color scheme in the bedroom. So I ripped out the bedspread and reused the yarn." The next slide featured his three adolescent sons sporting sweaters made from the brown acrylic yarn. Max said, "My sons really didn't like to wear the sweaters and pretty soon they grew out of them." He clicked to the third slide, "As you can see, the sweaters were unraveled and I made vests for my sons and their wives." Six sorrowful faces looked out from the screen. "It was just a matter of time before my sons and their wives began to have children. I took that brown yarn and knit up some baby hats for my grandchildren." It was at this point that I began to marvel at the strength of acrylic and at Max's refusal to let any scrap of yarn go to waste.

Max told us he learned to knit while stationed in a small French village during World War II. "There was nothing to do but wait for the Nazis to invade. So the French women invited the U.S. soldiers into their homes to drink tea and knit socks." Max saw little action during his tour of duty but he got a solid education in knitting, purling, and reusing yarn.

The second session of my knitting class began with a lesson in casting on. I remember how awkward my fingers felt and how the yarn and needles felt totally out of control. I had a difficult time believing people actually attempted this craft for relaxation. I likened it to learning to drive—at first it takes your total concentration but eventually the motions become automatic and you sink into a Zen-like state. I kept telling myself I would get the hang of knitting. The bonus was that, unlike driving, a mistake would not kill anyone and my injuries would be contained to the wrist and hand area.

Max told us our first project would be a simple scarf. The edges would be done in seed stitch and the body of the scarf in stockinet. I decided I would use my rose-colored acrylic yarn to make a scarf for my Grandma Peg. The weeks went by and I actually made progress on the scarf. I dropped stitches, purled when I should have knit, and had uneven tension—but still it was progress. The act of knitting quickly became a bit addictive. "Just one more row—Just one more row" became my catch phrase.

The last class was show-and-tell day. Some of the students had dropped out and others did not finish their projects. For those of us who caught the knitting bug, it was a fun session. Max beamed as we showed the class our handiwork. He told us we were beginning a lifelong passion and that our knitting would only improve with practice and time. As we filed out of class into the hallway, Max bellowed after us, "Remember, if you're not entirely happy with your scarves you can rip them out and start again!" I guess that comment sums up Max's philosophy on life. In my last glimpse of him I noticed Max was wearing a brown handknitted tie.

I presented the scarf to my grandmother. Her eyes filled with tears and for once she was speechless. She pronounced it "too good to wear" and lovingly placed it on the back of her favorite easy chair. She said it would remain there so she could brag to visitors about her talented granddaughter. I told her I wanted her to wear the scarf, but in spite of her promises I knew she probably never would. She didn't want to risk it being damaged by a falling snowflake or raindrop. It was one of those treasured things she wanted to hold close to her heart.

As Max promised, my knitting improved with time and practice. I hit some big stumbling blocks along the way. There was the major gauge mistake that resulted in a baby hat big enough to cover a watermelon. I made a batch of felted mittens one Christmas that turned out so pointy the recipients dubbed them "Grinch Gloves" in honor of the slender-fingered Dr. Seuss character.

I took many classes at my local yarn shop and my skills improved. Soon I was attacking cables and bobbles with gusto. I could actually hold two colors of yarn in two hands. As I began to go beyond knitting basic garments, I realized my knitting projects were a way for me to get in touch with my grandmothers and my heritage. The storytelling cables and stitches in Aran sweaters reminded me of my Irish grandmother, Peg. A friend got me skeins of yarn from Ireland's Dingle Peninsula. The bits of straw in the yarn and its sheepy smell were a conduit for my senses to experience the land my grandmother spoke of fondly.

My latest project, a Norwegian sweater, reminds me of my Swedish American grandmother, Flo. Like her, it is precise and requires great attention to detail. If you tackle a Norwegian sweater, you cannot be sloppy and must obey the rules—a sentiment Flo would heartily approve of.

My knitting is a way for me to celebrate my roots and to remember two strong women. I've had the pleasure of teaching a few people to knit. I enjoy sharing the story of how I learned the skill from a World War II veteran obsessed with taking things that no longer work and making them into something useful—a lesson that's good to practice even if you never pick up a knitting needle. Just try to stay away from the brown acrylic, because you'll be living with it for the rest of your life!

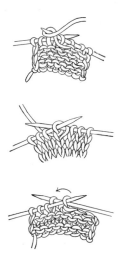

Chapter 2

BABY NEEDS A NEW PAIR OF . . .

"I WAS SO GRATEFUL—FOR THE FACT OF THE BABIES AS MUCH AS FOR THEIR APPARENT COMPLETENESS AND THE ABSENCE OF LASTING DAMAGE TO THEIR MOTHERS—THAT I WAS SEIZED WITH A DESIRE TO GIVE THEM SOMETHING, SOMETHING THAT MIGHT MANAGE TO CONVEY EVEN ONE SMALL PARTICLE OF THAT GRATITUDE. THE ONLY WAY I KNEW OF TO DO THAT WAS TO MAKE SOMETHING. THE ONLY WAY TO MAKE SOMETHING THAT SEEMED AT ALL APPROPRIATE WAS WITH KNITTING."

—*Lela Nargi,* Knitting Lessons: Tales from the Knitting Path, *2003*

As anyone who's tried it understands, knitting baby items can be a tricky endeavor. Many times, the knitter begins the project without knowing if the baby is a girl or a boy, so selecting an appropriate pattern and color can be a challenge. If the sweater, cap, or booties take longer than anticipated, there's always the chance that the baby will outgrow the gift before it is finished. And then, if something should go wrong during the pregnancy . . . well, one hates to think about it, but it does happen. What to do? On the following pages, knitters relate the often emotional ups and downs of knitting baby items and what they discover about themselves along the way.

THE WILL TO KNIT

BY KARI CORNELL

In "The Will to Knit," writer and new mom Kari Cornell gives a play-by-play of her race to complete a complicated Solveig Hisdal cardigan for her baby boy before he outgrows it. Kari has been knitting for four years and she is the editor of *For the Love of Knitting: A Celebration of the Knitter's Art.*

My husband Brian and I had just returned from a trip to New Orleans when we found out we were expecting a baby. The news was thrilling, since we had been planning to start a family for some time. But rather than throw myself into the frenzy of preparing the nursery, shopping for baby gear, and knitting a layette, I found myself wandering around in a fog of disbelief. We went shopping for a daybed for our bedroom the day the home pregnancy test showed a positive result. As we walked through one living room display after another at Room and Board, more than once I tugged on Brian's sleeve and asked with glee, "Can you believe we're going to have a baby?!" When we returned home, I looked again at the double lines on the testing wand—I had been so giddy about the results that I saved the test, setting it on the medicine-cabinet shelf, much like a proud parent posts a child's "A" paper on the fridge. Sure enough, the tiny pink lines were still there. . . . I *was* pregnant.

Being first-time parents and somewhat skeptical as to whether or not this pregnancy thing was actually going to stick, we made the decision not to tell anyone until we safely entered the second trimester. That meant struggling through Thanksgiving and Christmas celebrations without blurting out the news. By New Year's Eve, the night we began telling our friends, I could barely contain myself. I could finally explain why I was so darned tired all of the time, and I was free to compare notes with girlfriends about their newborns.

Most importantly, I could begin to knit something for the little guy or gal without worrying about revealing our secret. It quickly became clear, however, that I was not one of those women suddenly struck with the urge to knit during pregnancy. In addition to feelings of exhaustion and queasiness, one of my early pregnancy symptoms was a lack of desire to knit. Over the long holiday weekends, which my pre-pregnant self would have savored as prime knitting time, I sunk into a slothlike state, lounging on my parent's couch and watching one movie after another.

My mom and I did take a trip to the local yarn shop once. Mom, who hadn't knit since before I was born, was interested in picking it up again and I was more than willing to teach her. I had high hopes that having something new to do with her hands might prompt her to give up smoking, but I had no such luck. She is still knitting, but also still smoking—although fortunately not at the same time. Anyway, I was thinking the trip to the yarn shop might be just the ticket: the allure of new yarn in a bevy of brilliant colors might bring forth my itch to knit. It didn't. My knitting bag remained untouched all weekend in the backseat of the cold car.

I was beginning to worry. Over the past few years, I knit half a dozen tiny caps to warm the heads of my friends' newborns, but I was on a sweater kick lately, and I wanted to knit the most beautiful sweater for my little one. A hat or a pair of adorable booties wouldn't do. But how could I possibly expect to finish an entire sweater, even a baby-sized one, when I had no desire to knit?

– – – –

As December slipped into January and January ebbed into February, Brian and I spent Friday nights snuggled up on the new daybed in the bedroom, watching old movies. We ate popcorn, drank steaming cups of hot chocolate, and read to each other from the many baby books that friends and relatives sent after we shared the good news. Never once while we were watching movies did I pick up my knitting needles.

To my credit, I did spend a lot of time *thinking* about what to knit for the baby. A coworker brought in a copy of Solveig Hisdal's *Poetry in Stitches*, and I was entranced by her lovely floral-patterned sweaters inspired by antique tapestries or the designs carved and painted on ancient Scandinavian artifacts. A complicated toddler sweater knit in gold, China blue, sage green, and cream with a dab of pink and red along the edges caught my eye. The bold, happy colors seemed like the perfect anecdote to the cold, dreary days of late winter in Minnesota and provided a cheerful counterpoint to my last project—an Icelandic Lopi sweater I knit for Brian in subdued browns, tans, and grays.

I really wanted to knit the Hisdal sweater, but I hesitated. I had never done such elaborate colorwork before, and I was intimidated by the size 2 and 3 needles—especially after just finishing the Lopi sweater on 10s. But both of these hurdles could be overcome. I liked the challenge the colorwork would provide and I felt I was ready to tackle it. I could get used to the smaller needles; I knit many of those early baby hats on 3¼-inch needles, and a size 3 needle wasn't much smaller.

I stopped at a local yarn shop on my way home from work one day. My intent was to buy some baby-friendly wool and begin the Hisdal sweater. Instead, I stumbled upon the most adorable baby hat, knit in a variegated cotton yarn. I couldn't resist. I knit one of the caps for a coworker whose wife was expecting a baby in a few weeks. The other went to a friend whose baby was already eighteen months old. You see, I have a history of unfinished knitted gifts and unfulfilled promises. I originally set out, more than six months before her baby was born, to knit this friend a baby blanket of multicolored squares. I abandoned that project after realizing the squares were all different sizes and the blanket would never come together in the tidy way I'd envisioned. The multicolored cap was my feeble attempt to save face.

The downward spiral had begun. My brother's birthday was coming up, so I rushed to knit him a cap too— only I used a different yarn than what was called for in the

- - - -

pattern and the hat turned out gigantic. Since it was all wool, I thought I'd try felting it. It did shrink up, but oddly so—it looked like something a troll would wear. And it took forever to dry. I ended up packing the thing in a Ziplock bag and sending it a week late. He claimed he liked it, but I'm guessing he never wears it. Sigh.

The sweater, the sweater . . . I had to get going on that sweater. But my mind still wandered. The baby was due in July, and surely a baby born in midsummer didn't need more than a drawerful of onesies and some diapers for the first few months. So if I wanted to knit the baby a sweater, I would have at least a year, maybe even a year and a half to finish it. That should give me plenty of time.

What a summer baby would need more than a sweater would be a nice, lightweight baby blanket, one that I could spread out on the lawn to give the baby a soft bed on which to sleep as I dawdled in the garden on summer mornings (I kid you not—this was but one of the many pastoral, totally unrealistic thoughts that clouded my brain throughout my pregnancy). I found a basic, garter-stitch blanket with a darling sawtooth edging in a Debbie Bliss book, and I marked the page.

Brian and I decided not to find out if the baby was a boy or a girl. Not knowing was fun, but it made knitting for the baby more of a challenge. Sure, there are always the unisex colors of yellow, green, and red available to knitters faced with this untimely dilemma. All three of these colors made an appearance in the sweater pattern in one shade or another, and I was confident that the color scheme would work for a boy or a girl. What I was most concerned about were the intricate flowers that danced across the lower part of the sweater's body and sleeves and that hint of pink picot trim that formed the sweater's bottom edge. These were the very details that had drawn me to the sweater in the first place, but I was having second thoughts. Would the sweater be too feminine for a boy?

Brian reassured me that the sweater would work for a boy or a girl and prodded me to get knitting, as, sooner than we realized, we'd be parents. At this point, half of February had passed me by, and I had not knit a stitch. I had President's Day off, so I headed to my favorite local yarn shop. The kind woman behind the counter pointed me in the direction of the thinly spun baby wool called for in the pattern, and I began to pull the blue, green, gold, red, and cream skeins from the shelves. In my arms, the bright colors seemed to cozy up to one another playfully, and I thought of the baby I'd soon cradle in much the same way, a baby dressed in the sweater I was about to knit. While I was there, I picked up enough light green yarn for that Debbie Bliss blanket, thinking an easy project would be a nice break from the more complicated sweater.

Back home, I made myself a cup of peppermint tea and snuggled into the corner of the couch in our home office, crossing my legs under me. This was my favorite place to knit, where I could stitch away and chat with Brian as he worked. Casting on with the soft, pink yarn reminded me that spring was right around the corner. Yes, these colors would certainly carry me through the last dreary days of winter. As the tiny pink ribbing took shape on my number 2 circular needles, I felt good about my decision to knit the sweater.

I made steady progress on the sweater in those first few weeks. A car trip to Davenport, Iowa, to attend my brother's long-overdue college graduation gave me twelve solid hours of knitting time. By the time we arrived, I had finished the pink picot edge, and the creamy, white leaves and stems of the flower "seedlings" began to sprout in a field of sage green. It seemed right to be knitting this garden in early spring, when a new life was growing inside me.

As I knit around in a circle, each stitch became a day in this sweater's growing season. The plants grew to their full height, pushing up through a band of China blue. Sometime in the month of May, under the gentle guidance of my knitting needles, the flowers bloomed before a glorious gold backdrop. With the flowers behind me, I focused on the repeated half moon pattern that reverberated like waves from the top of the blooms to the sweater's neckline. The rest should be a breeze, I thought.

But soon it was early summer, and we were busy registering for baby items and attending showers thoughtfully thrown by friends and family. My knitting bag was always at hand as we traveled to each event. Looking for an easy fix and thinking I might actually be able to finish one project for the baby before he or she came into the world, I often reached for the Debbie Bliss blanket. The garter stitch was effortless, and I didn't have to constantly consult the pattern or cradle a knitting book on my lap as I worked. I made progress on the blanket as the sweater languished in my knitting bag. I always brought the sweater along, though, in case I suddenly had the urge to work on it. And I loved to show off my handiwork. At my extended-family shower, I ran to fetch the sweater from the car so that I could show it to my maternal grandmother.

"It's kind of feminine," I explained, "but I really love the pattern."

"It's beautiful, Kari. You've really done a nice job," she said.

I beamed as I carefully folded the sweater and placed it back in my bag. But not before my paternal grandmother offered her opinion from the other side of the room.

"That looks like a girl's sweater," she said.

My smile faded. What if we did have a boy? Would I still dress him in the sweater? Old doubts resurfaced as I recalled a conversation I'd had with friends at my knitting club's March meeting. I had decided to ask these women, friends I always know I can confide in and trust, what they thought of the sweater. The first time I pulled the sweater from my bag, they praised my work and admired my courage for taking on such a daunting project. That should have been enough; I should have kept my mouth shut, picked up the needles, and begun to knit. But as usual, I couldn't leave well enough alone. The question leaped from my lips, as if it had a mind of its own.

"You don't think it's too feminine, do you?" I asked.

"No, not for a baby," one friend volunteered.

"Well, if he's under a year old, it shouldn't matter," another friend replied, "but it is pretty feminine."

Uh-oh. I had selected the pattern in part because it was

– – – –

designed to fit kids between the ages of one and two, giving me a year or two to complete the sweater, a time frame that had seemed perfectly manageable. I focused on my knitting as I listened to the ensuing discussion. One friend after another lamented about how difficult it can be to get a kid to wear something as basic as a plain t-shirt. This was not what I wanted to hear—not about what was to come for the little angel I'd be bringing in to the world, and not about this knitting project. But I had always been stubborn. I continued knitting the sweater.

When these same friends threw me a shower, I was blown away by the beautiful gifts, many of them handmade. I received a lovely, cream-colored baby blanket, knit from a silk blend in an intricate lace pattern; a darling purple cap; an adorable green cardigan with white star buttons; and a colorful crib quilt in a vintage pattern. I was in awe of my friends' craftiness, but also of their ability to finish projects in enough time for the recipient to enjoy them— something I seemed unable to accomplish.

With the showers and other baby-centered events behind us, we hunkered down during that first weekend in July, scrambling to move our TV room from the third bedroom to the unfinished basement to make way for the baby. Unlike my knitting projects, the room came together just

– – – –

as we had envisioned it. On the wall above the crib hung an old patchwork quilt that I had picked up for five bucks at an auction. But the main attraction was an old dresser my mom had painted with brightly colored fairy-tale animals. It was perfect.

After filling the dresser with neatly stacked piles of freshly laundered baby clothes, I packed my bag for the hospital. I had to remember to bring my knitting, I thought. It would be nice to have something on which to focus as I worked through the contractions.

What kind of insane notion was that?

I began having contractions the day after we finished the baby's room. From the time they began until my water broke three days later(!), I was in no mood to knit. In fact, all the comfort measures I thought I would need in the hospital—essential oils, music, my knitting—remained in my overnight bag because our baby was born a mere hour and a half after we arrived at the hospital. And it was funny—after all the time I spent worrying about whether we would have a boy or girl while I was knitting during my pregnancy, the baby's sex was an afterthought in the delivery room. I was tired and relieved when the nurse placed our baby in my arms for the first time. We named him William Edward, and we couldn't have been happier.

– – – –

Three days after Will was born, my mom came to visit. She presented me with a cute little light green baby cardigan and cap, knit from a pattern I picked out months earlier. She used a different yarn than what was called for in the pattern, and the results were fantastic. I was impressed. How ironic that I taught her to knit just eight months earlier and here she was already dressing her grandchild in garments she knit herself while I only completed four inches of the sweater I was knitting. And the compliments that sweater draws! Every time he wears it someone comments on how cute the set is, and then asks if I knit it myself. I smile and tell them that his grandma knit it for him, but inside I'm gritting my teeth. If I could only finish that sweater!

Will is now almost six months old, and the sweater is still very much a work in progress. (I gave up on the blanket months ago, after receiving about twenty of them as shower gifts.) My three-month maternity leave came and went so quickly it seems like a dream. "All that time" I thought I'd have to sit on the patio, sipping lemonade, and knitting away on the sweater (to say nothing of dawdling in the garden) turned out to be no time at all.

What time I did have was spent nursing the baby. At

- - - -

one point it occurred to me that I should try knitting while feeding Will. A friend from my knitting club once provided tips on knitting while nursing. She claimed she was able to feed her baby and knit while lying in bed. The key, she said, was to knit with circular needles, as straights posed a poking hazard. That sounded like an Olympic event to me, one for which I definitely was not qualified. But the sweater was on circulars, so I gave it a try, sitting up of course. It didn't work. Any time Will flinched or shifted I struggled to keep him on the nursing pillow, usually jockeying him back into place with my elbows and often losing stitches in the process. Knitting and nursing just wasn't for me.

Our son is beautiful, and I love him dearly, but I'd be lying if I said I wasn't a little concerned about finishing the sweater. It's December and I'm two inches shy of completing the body, with the two sleeves yet to knit. Little Will is growing so fast I can almost see it happen. Meanwhile, my friend's comment about how picky one-year-old boys can be about clothes keeps ringing in my ears. And, it turns out two of the friends who knit such lovely gifts for Will are pregnant. Looks as if I won't be finishing that sweater anytime soon. . . .

THE PERFECT BABY HAT

by Amy Votava

Often the creative process begins with an idealistic vision of the completed project, but realizing that dream, in all of its flawlessness, can be challenging, if not impossible. In "The Perfect Baby Hat," author Amy Votava comes to terms with her quest for perfection in her knitting projects and in her everyday life. Amy is a writer who lives in Minneapolis, Minnesota, with her husband David, her daughter Olivia, and her son Isaiah. She is currently working on her MFA in creative writing at Hamline University. Knitting with her knitting group is one of Amy's favorite ways to take a break from her studies.

For months now I've been envisioning knitting the perfect baby hat. It's adorable, of course, but the details are still fuzzy. The hat will have some kind of polka-dot theme—you know, something dazzling and whimsical. I'll

- - - -

use the softest yarn I can find, the kind that people will pick up and touch and remark, "Oh, it's just so soft!" The colors will be gender neutral, since I don't yet know the sex of my baby, who will be born in just three months. I'm thinking of a buttery yellow combined with a soft green. This sounds delightful, but there's just one problem.

I can hardly knit.

Oh, I've been at it a while, all right. But I'm not the most patient person on the planct. I joined a knitting group about a year ago, and I love it, but we only meet once every month or so. And whenever I sit down to knit in between our gatherings, I end up skipping a stitch and then trying to undo it, and then trying to move on anyway in spite of the mistake, and then trying to get my cat to stop attacking the yarn, and then trying to untangle the yarn, and then trying to explain to my six year old why I can't teach her to knit just now, and then the phone rings, and, well, you get the picture. I'm nowhere near able to produce the hat I've just described.

There's a loud voice inside me that says, "Oh, just give it up and go buy a handknit hat at a store!" Or, better yet, I think, maybe one of my many skilled knitting friends will give me a hat as a present and I can, you know, pretend that

I made myself. But of course I wouldn't do that. Besides, there's also this little, weak voice inside me, let's call it the voice of reason, that is gently suggesting, "Can't you just adjust your expectations a bit? I mean, how about a simple stockinet-stitched tube in a solid color that you can cinch at the top?"

I want to listen to this voice. I truly do. But there's one problem; this step closer to reality makes all the fuzzy details disappear. I can see it perfectly now, the simple little hat with uneven stitching and mistakes all over it. After all, I make the same mistakes that most beginning knitters make—I split the yarn and can't undo it, in my zeal sometimes I use too much tension and then I overcompensate and knit too loosely for several rows. The result is often an uneven mess. But why not try anyway? Why not just shrug my shoulders and knit the hat anyway?

When I think about my dilemma with the baby hat, I can't help but be reminded of my catapult into motherhood six years ago. The unrealistic picture I had of parenting wasn't so unlike the unrealistic vision that I have of the adorable baby hat. As I walked around all glowing and round, in expectation of my first child, all sorts of scenes of what parenting would be like played out before me, all of them blissful and all of them involving perfection.

As my baby turned and gave me gentle kicks, I rubbed my belly and pictured myself writing peacefully at the computer while my infant slept soundly next to me in a bassinette. I reached out every now and then and rocked my baby, sighed with admiration, and then went back to work. I'm a lover of nature, so sometimes I imagined my child and myself lying in the yard with a magnifying glass, exploring the insect world below the grass.

I pictured myself as the natural earth-mother type— happy, calm, patient, whistling away while I ground up my own organic baby food and threw another load of cloth diapers into the washer. I actually remember telling my husband, "I will never use the word 'no' with our child. Instead, I'll just explain patiently why something isn't a good idea." He smiled and agreed and I sat back and imagined how perfect motherhood was going to be.

I was that clueless.

In reality, my beautiful infant daughter had colic and often cried and fussed for four hours straight. I sighed all right, but not as I sat peacefully rocking her in a bassinette.

- - - -

Instead, I sighed and paced the floor and sighed and paced the floor, crying right along with her as I soaked my pajamas with breast milk. I did make my own organic baby food, and enjoyed it, but the cloth diapers didn't last long. And little did I know that my toddler would rather smash a bug dead with her foot than lay still and observe it. And, one time, when my four-year-old daughter was overtired and cranky, screaming that she wanted to be picked up and then screaming that she wanted to be put back down and then screaming that she wanted a particular toy and then throwing it at me, and then hitting me, not only did I scream "NO!" but I swore at her, stormed out of the kitchen, and slammed the door. Hard.

To my credit, I did calm down rather quickly. I apologized to my daughter, talked to her about her feelings and what would have been appropriate behavior, and put her down for a long nap. But then I called a friend and left a desperate message—a dire need to talk. She called me right back.

"Talk to me," she said.

I told her exactly what I did, not watering it down at all.

"I behaved horribly," I told my friend. "It wasn't pretty."

What I was telling her felt a lot bigger than just a detailed account of an incident. It felt more like a confession. The message behind the message was clear, heart wrenching, and scary. Basically, what I was telling her was this: "There is no perfection. I'm not the perfect mother and I don't have a perfect child." My friend echoed my thoughts exactly. It was eerie.

"Amy," she said, "You're not perfect. There's a limit to how much you can take because you're human."

When I hung up, I felt so much better, and my vision, not unlike my vision of knitting the perfect baby hat, was so much clearer. I looked back honestly on the previous four years, with all the holes and unevenness and imperfection and charm and beauty and well, downright, bug-smashing realness.

As far as this new baby goes, I'm excited, but I don't have the illusions of perfection anymore. Obviously, there are still sugary and unrealistic thoughts lurking there under the surface and I think those thoughts are embodied in this perfect baby hat. But I've taken an important first step. Since starting this essay, I've contacted a friend who's a knitter and asked her to teach me to knit a nice little hat for my new baby. I didn't hold back. "I can do a knit stitch and I can kind of purl stitch. Oh, and I'm a horrible kinesthetic learner. Oh yeah, and I can't follow a pattern either."

– – – –

I can't wait for my first knitting lesson, and, to tell you truth, I'm getting more comfortable with the vision of the little rag-tag hat that will keep my baby's head warm. After all, the other day my daughter ran into the kitchen, all out of breath and yelled, "Mommy, mommy, you have to come quick! It's so cool! It's just so COOL!" We ran out into the sunshine together, hand in hand, letting the screen door slam behind us. She pulled me across the yard and crouched down and craned her neck forward to watch a black speck on her plastic slide. I crouched down with her and there, before us both, was a perfectly still cicada, ready to shed its skin. "We should leave it alone," she whispered, "We don't want to scare it." She's come a long way from the bug-squashing toddler she used to be. We've come a long way. Life is like this, I guess: the perfection and joy woven in tightly with the mistakes and the tears.

When my baby is born and I put my first real knitting project on his or her little precious head, perhaps I can think of it as a symbol for how all mothers hand themselves over to their children. For better or worse, this hat will proclaim, here I am. I'll try my best for you and our experience together will have all the contradictions of real life—unique but common, beautiful but scarred, imperfect but, in many ways, absolutely perfect.

– – – –

THE MYSTERIOUS STITCH

BY CARRIE MERCER

During a particularly difficult time in her own life, author Carrie Mercer found solace in the act of knitting stuffed bears for orphaned and abandoned children in Africa. Carrie Mercer writes a column for *Cablegram,* the newsletter of the Minnesota Knitters' Guild, and is a book reviewer for the literary magazine *Rain Taxi*. She holds an MFA from Hamline University, and has worked as a writing consultant. Carrie has published poetry for both children and adults, and has been a judge for the Minnesota Book Awards.

Before I lost the baby I had never knit in my life. There are no knitters in my family. Becoming pregnant did not suddenly create in me a desire to take up knitting. Knitting wasn't even on my radar. I was busy finishing a thesis for my master's degree, and planning my new role in life as Mom. I planned to make a smooth transition from being Writer/Master's Student to Writer/Mom. Everything was finally in place.

- - - -

After five years of trying, my husband and I had at long last been able to conceive through IVF. Months of shots, pills, tests, patience, and hope had produced a positive pregnancy test. At six weeks, just after Christmas, we saw the baby's heartbeat on ultrasound. Nothing had ever looked so amazing. I kept a journal of the changes I knew were happening, both the ones I felt and the ones I read about— I found tidbits like "this week your baby is as big as a pea" completely engrossing. I wanted to write a book about the relatively short but transformative state of being pregnant, so I took as many notes as I could, often while lying on my side fighting morning sickness. At three months, we started telling family the good news, thinking we were safely out of the danger zone of the first trimester. Two weeks later, disaster struck.

The day of the miscarriage was not the hardest day to live through. That day I was too busy to feel the full impact of my loss. Too busy with the tragedy itself. Not five minutes after I got up that morning, I felt the unmistakable gush of my water breaking. I ran to the bathroom. Then came the blood: warm, red, and nonstop.

Do not panic, I told myself firmly, do not lose it. Find the phone number of the clinic. Dial the number. The clinic is closed, you are too early. Do not panic. Listen for the other number on the recording. Dial that number. Now listen to the nurse: listen to what she is saying, try to focus, try to hear her, and tune everything else out. Do not think about what is happening, do not think about this, that you are losing the baby. Do not think. Just listen. She is telling you to call 911. She is telling you no, you do not have time to call your husband at work and have him come home to take you to the hospital. You do not have time. You are losing too much blood. You could go into shock and pass out. Hang up now. Call 911.

Now you must go downstairs and unlock the front door so that if you do pass out, the paramedics can get in and find you. You need to find some clothes to wear to the hospital—not something new like you'd planned. Just something. Anything.

Now you are in the ambulance and the paramedic is telling you that you are probably having a miscarriage. It happens a lot. It's not that unusual. He is not helping.

In the hospital, they stick you with needles, one IV in each arm. You keep still but you scream because it hurts, everything hurts. You are cramping now, and it hurts more than cramps have ever hurt. These are your contractions, the nurse is telling you, these are your birth contractions. She asks if you need more pain medication and you say yes, you think so. You don't know.

- - - -

You look for your husband. You look for his face and try to focus on his face and shut out everything else.

"We'll be okay, right?" you ask him, "We'll be okay even though we lost the baby?"

"We'll be okay," he says, nodding his head, squeezing your hand. He leaves for a while, and the nurse says he is lying down in another room; he felt dizzy like he was going to pass out. Bring him back, you say, bring him back to me.

And it goes on like that: tests, needles, blood, doctors, nurses . . . for eight hours.

Finally it is over. The baby is gone and they send us home. And I am exhausted. For a few days I am relieved just to be alive, and we hold on to each other and appreciate that.

Then starts the hard part: living through the quiet emptiness after the crisis is over. I find I can't sit up for more than a few minutes at a time or I'll start to pass out. They didn't say how long this would last, or what to do next. What to do?

After a week we decide we must give the baby a name. We choose Miranda, after Prospero's daughter in *The Tempest*. Upon seeing other people for the first time, she is full of joy and wonder, saying "O brave new world, that has such people in't!" The promise of this baby created for us a

_ _ _ _

brave new world, and even though she is gone, we will never be the same.

I rest a lot, curled up under blankets in the middle of an already dreary February made even drearier by this sudden, inexplicable loss. I wish there was something I could do, especially with my hands. They suddenly feel so strange, so inadequate. I am like a performer with stage fright, suddenly aware of her hands, unable to put them anywhere that feels natural.

I try watching movies. I try reading. Usually this works, losing myself in a story, but not this time. After a few minutes my mind drifts away from the scene; my hands drop the book. I can't seem to engage with characters: I can't care about their lives, their troubles, their joys. I want to stop thinking about losing Miranda, to stop crying, to stop feeling hollowed out. At the same time, I don't want to stop thinking about her. It feels like a betrayal to invest myself in any other story but Miranda's. I rest my hands on my belly and take deep breaths.

Even though I hadn't started showing by the time I lost Miranda, I had already begun to cradle in my hands that space where I knew she floated. Sometimes I ran my hands over my expanding belly, trying to calm the rising nausea of morning sickness, or just trying to feel myself fitting

– – – –

into this new role I had finally achieved: Mom. Now that she is gone, my hands feel useless. I wasn't able to protect my child with them, and now it seems all they can cradle is this terrible tragedy and my powerlessness to stop it.

My hands physically ache for something purposeful to do. Weeks pass like years. Then one morning a photo of a knit teddy bear catches my eye in the newspaper. The Mother Bear Project, a charity started by a local mom, is meeting at a St. Paul bookstore. If you show up to help, they will teach you how to knit. I read the article over and over, still having trouble focusing. I feel fragile and lost in the world. But I do know this bookstore. Finally I decide I will go. When I arrive, there are about thirty women present, and I sit down with them and listen to a woman named Amy explain how she got started with this project. The bears are for orphaned and abused children in Africa. She wants them to have a little comfort, and something to call their own. The patterns are easy, she says, and the bears don't have to be perfect. Each will be different, unique. She holds up some completed bears and the women around me ooh and aah over them.

I buy my first pair of knitting needles, fourteen-inch-long Susan Bates #7s in slippery blue metal. The yarn is free, all donated, and I get to choose three different colored yarns for my bear. It's like choosing which crayons to color with—important and not important at the same time. There is no wrong color.

An experienced knitter sitting beside me volunteers to teach me. She puts her hands over mine and guides me through the long-tail cast-on. I practice it over and over. It's like laying the foundation of a building. A little tight, she says. But I want it to be secure. So we move on to the knit stitch, to using both needles. It's very exciting—and also horribly awkward. I want it to just come to me, the flowing motion I see in the other women's hands around me. I want it to be like the dreams I have where I can play the piano just by willing my hands and having the intent to make something beautiful. Instead I feel like a monkey learning to type. But I'm not discouraged. No one is making fun of the monkey. So I focus carefully on each stitch, following the sequence I have been taught—pushing the working needle through the first stitch on the needle that's holding the cast-on stitches, wrapping the strand of yarn from the ball around the working needle, then somehow pushing and pulling to bring the new yarn through the old, and finally moving the old stitch off the holder needle. The hardest part is the last step, moving the old stitch all the way off the needle, letting it fall, trusting it will be held in

- - - -

place by the new stitch I have just worked above it. I like seeing the stitches *on* the needle: they look so neat and ordered, all standing at attention. It seems such a shame to disturb them. But when I finally finish the first row of ten stitches, I am ecstatic.

The next mystery is solved when my teacher shows me how to switch the needles between my hands and position them to start a new row. And look—there they are again, the neat little soldiers, all standing at attention! I wonder how I will ever remember all this.

At one point I somehow yank the yarn and the whole piece slips off the needle onto the floor. Horrors! Cartoon visions of unraveling fabric fill my head, an entire sweater reduced to a pile of string in mere seconds. But nothing happens; it just lies there on the rug. My teacher calmly places the stitches back on the needle and I am able to continue. Later I make a mistake and she shows me how to undo what I have done so I can do it over correctly. I feel much calmer then, knowing I have the power to do it over if something goes wrong.

After two hours, the meeting is over, and I have about half of one leg done on my first bear. It looks like a tiny accomplishment, but it feels huge. This little leg is the beginning of something that, in my hands, under my power,

- - - -

will grow and ultimately be complete. For the first time since the miscarriage, I feel like I might be something more than just the woman who lost her baby.

Hours pass, days begin and end, and for a while, this is all I can do, and all I want to do: knit. There is something addictive about it, and I do not get tired of it. Knitting, I find, is that act that fits where I need it to—into my grief. The other things I'd tried—reading, watching movies—are distractions from the grief, but in knitting, I do not have to set aside the hurt. I can knit through it. Getting through the grief is like taking a long road trip: it's not about getting there quickly, but more about the slow, steady movement of miles passing. The changes in the landscape are so gradual, I may not even realize I am adjusting to them. In knitting, I find this same steady movement. So I fill the miles of grief with knitting, and like miles, the stitches gradually accumulate.

It takes me more than a month and another meeting to finish my first Mother Bear. It's an incredible feeling to have finished, to have made something whole. I struggle with the fact that I lacked the power to save Miranda, so it's a wonderful contrast to have the power to create this bear. He is a little lopsided, because after the first half I began to feel confident that the stitches really would hold together, and I stopped knitting so tightly. A couple of months later, I finish my second bear and sign Miranda's name to it, sending my love for her out into the world instead of holding it all inside. It feels good.

Two years, dozens of needles, and a room full of yarn later, I am still knitting, and not just to get through hard times. Creating something from nothing more than colorful string and a couple of sticks—it's downright magical. More than that, there is something hypnotic, meditative, even prayerful, about working with my hands, and I don't like to go a whole day without knitting. Learning to knit reminded me that life will always get bigger again, no matter what happens. Like the five different knitting projects I am always in the middle of, I am not yet done becoming. The biggest surprise to me is, as excited as I am to finish that bear or sock or hat or sweater, I still find the deepest satisfaction in the process itself—the flowing motion of my hands, the click of the needles, and the reassuring accumulation of one mysterious stitch after another.

❋ For more information on the Mother Bear Project, visit www.Motherbear.org.

Faith, Hope, and Knitting

by Betty Christiansen

Every stitch of the blanket Betty Christiansen knits in "Faith, Hope, and Knitting" holds the hope that the blanket will one day cuddle her own baby. Betty Christiansen is a freelance editor and writer who has knitted since the age of eight and whose writing about knitting has appeared in several magazines and books, including *For the Love of Knitting: A Celebration of the Knitter's Art,* published by Voyageur Press in 2004, and Melanie Falick's *Handknit Holidays*, published by Stewart, Tabori & Chang in 2005. Betty is currently at work on her first book for Stewart, Tabori & Chang. She has an MFA in nonfiction writing from Sarah Lawrence College and lives with her husband in the Mississippi River valley of southeastern Minnesota.

– – – –

If dreams could be made real on needles, like the baby blanket I am knitting, we'd have the house by now. It would be as real as the squares spread out on my coffee table, simple stockinet blocks I've knit almost without thinking. I had always believed the right house would come to me nearly as effortlessly—one walk through it and I'd know I was home. Something about it—a pleasing nook, a fall of light—would signal that I belonged there, that my husband and I would be happy there, that in it we might raise a family. The house we've found isn't really it, but we've placed an offer on it anyway, in faith that it might be close enough.

I catch myself wandering through the house in my mind, one room at a time. I begin in the foyer, with the peeling wallpaper that we'll have to take down and the yellowed carpet we'll have to take up, and I head right up the stairs. It's a grand staircase, though the baseboards all need refinishing and we're sure the banister isn't original. There's a stained-glass window at the top. The landing is vast, like a room in itself, and it's here, I've decided, I'll put my spinning wheel—here, where the evening light will land just so on my hands and the wool and the thrumming wheel. I pass the two smaller bedrooms—one with a porch, one with a fireplace—and enter the master bedroom, my favorite. It

– – – –

spans the entire front of the house. In the northeast corner, the one with the tower, I'll put my desk, and maybe the view, the angled windows, will inspire me to write. Our bed will go in the curtained nook, and in the sitting area outside—that's where we'll put the baby.

But the house, like the baby, is turning out to be elusive. We've been trying to buy it—a stately Victorian in La Crosse, Wisconsin—for months now, but an obstinate seller and his trickster agent are proving to be prohibitive. One closing has fallen through already—they hadn't bothered to ask the current renters to leave—and though another is scheduled for next week, our hopes aren't high. Still, the house sneaks into my thoughts. I buy shades for the tower window when I find them on sale; I bid on an iron bed frame for the guest room at an auction. And though it seems foolish, as though by doing so we are tempting fate, we buy a crib there, too—no one else wanted it. *If I paint it white, it'll go with the blanket,* I can't help but think. But that's getting ahead of things.

La Crosse is a charming Mississippi River city, with a resurrected historic downtown and just enough art and commerce to keep me happy. It's got coffee shops and a bookstore and two yarn shops, one of which I frequent at least once a week, when we gather for knitting nights. The group that meets there is intelligent and warm, prompting interesting and honest conversation. Still, La Crosse is small as cities go, and as these women know everyone in it (including my mother-in-law), I hedge from baring my heart. Some personal topics are safe for discussion, others are not. They all know about the house, for example, but I've never brought up the baby.

They ask, with hope-filled eyes and smiles, about the progress of the house every time I see them, and I'm honest about our struggles. If they inquired after the baby with the same intensity as they do the house, I could not bear it. The house I can chalk up to bad luck and someone else's incompetence. The baby, which has not come about because of a little ovulation problem, feels too much like a personal failure. I can let myself dream about the house—if the deal falls through, we can always find another. The same is not true of the baby.

It's November now, a darkening month, and a baby conceived now—like a bulb planted just before frost—will be born in August. I love the idea of a baby born in that ripe month, when red-winged blackbirds whirr a lullaby in the cattail swamps along the Mississippi, when trees cross to the other side of verdant, when the sun sets lush and crimson in the haze. If this is to be, however, time is of the essence. It is anyway; this year I turned thirty-five, crossing an invisible threshold to become "a woman of advanced maternal age," as I read somewhere recently. According to experts, my fertility is about to take a dive—it may have already—and my lack of ovulation, though treatable, they say, does not seem like a good sign.

I haven't waited this long by accident. At twenty-four, when many of my friends were marrying their boyfriends, I was breaking up with mine. I married at twenty-nine, when those same friends already had a child or two, and we promptly moved to New York for my grad-school pursuits. I came back to the Midwest at thirty-three, and we began the baby efforts shortly after. At no point have I felt a maternal urge; I've even questioned whether motherhood was the thing for me. "Your body will tell you when it's time," mother-friends assured me, but my body never has. It's the biological clock on which I've kept hitting "snooze" that's finally woken me up. The issue, now, is not whether I want a baby, but whether I'll ever be able to have one if I don't start trying.

So, as with the house, I don't think about it too hard, but blindly execute the appropriate actions, my husband's gentle assurance as my guide wire. I knit another square, secure financing, buy furniture, tear decorating ideas out

of magazines, take folic acid and the medication that's supposed to help me ovulate—all with the faith that with each
page, each signature, each square, each pill, I am doing what
small thing I can to ensure that our efforts will be rewarded.
Each step, however mundane or minute, is a prayer that
the house will work out, that the baby will be conceived,
and that I'll somehow be ready for it all when it happens.

I didn't start knitting the blanket with a baby in mind,
I just bought the yarn because I loved it—the buttery-soft
merino wool, the satisfaction of pulling together colors
pleasing to my eye, the simplicity of the blanket design. It's
a good mindless project for movie-watching or hours spent
talking long-distance, updating my sister Gwen in Michi-
gan on the baby issue (she's a new mother herself and a
veteran of my nonovulation problem), and complaining
about the house to my friend Melody in Connecticut. "It's
as if I just can't move forward," I protest, "no matter how
hard I try."

"But are you knitting?" Melody asks, over the click of
her own needles.

"Yes," I reply.

"Well, that's something," she says.

Melody was with me when I bought the baby-blanket
yarn, and I love her for not asking why or, the question I

used to get so frequently from my in-laws, *when*. I've noticed they haven't asked so much lately; my guess is that they're well aware of my age, and their hopes, like my fertility, are plummeting. I don't let on that we're trying, nor do I bring the blanket to my knitting nights. I keep this one thing private. I did tell a friend the other night, though, a woman who, thirty-five herself, just picked out a ring with her boyfriend. Unlike me, she has craved a child for years, and already has decorated a baby's room with teddy bears in her mind. "Have you thought about a nursery theme?" she asks when I confide to her my efforts.

"No," I say, a little surprised. "But I did start this blanket."

"Tell me about it," she says, and I describe it in detail: the simple patchwork design, the squares of rose and gold and cream and slate green—sophisticated and unexpected for a baby. And as I describe the blanket, my nursery theme materializes, too: it's hope, pure and simple. By knitting this blanket, as with the pill-taking and the house-dealing, I *am* moving forward, with quiet persistence and a seed of a dream, through uncertainty and genetics and plain bad luck. Each square is a hope that somewhere, some progress less obvious is being made. But it's also a statement: though some outcomes are beyond my control, others are not. As

- - - -

surely as I can knit this blanket, one square at a time, I can create a life that is meaningful and rich—without a baby, if that's how it must be, and certainly without this particular house. The blanket reminds me not to give up, that goals can be worked toward through doubt and fear. If I could surround a child or fill a home with any symbol of patience and faith, it would be this.

It's also a hope for happiness—that we will find a house we love, that I will be a good mother, that we will be a family, with children or not. It's a deep, blind faith in what has gone before and what is yet to be, a hope handed down, like an heirloom or like knitting itself, through long lines of women.

Row by mindless row, the blanket grows without my thinking about it, much like a baby would if there were one. This is a creative act of my own willing, though; this one *will* come to fruition, and if it doesn't wrap a baby of my own, it'll enfold someone else's, another one equally as dear.

– – – –

THE BABY BLUE BLANKIE

BY KAY DORN

In "The Baby Blue Blankie," writer Kay Dorn relates her tradition of knitting a special blanket for each of her grandchildren. Under tragic circumstances, one of the blankets ends up fulfilling an unexpected but very important role.

Kay recently retired from editing a business newspaper. She enjoys knitting for her grandchildren, going for walks with her husband, and volunteering at the library. Her essays have been published in *Knit Lit: Sweaters and Their Stories . . . and Other Writing about Knitting; KnitLit (too): Stories from Sheep to Shawl . . . and More Writing about Knitting;* and *For the Love of Knitting: A Celebration of the Knitter's Art.*

I'm a lucky grandmother—I've been able to enjoy knitting blankets for five grandchildren. But because I never knew which would be appropriate—pink or blue—they all had to be canary yellow, minty green, or mixed pastels. Then finally, for number six, we knew—the blankie could be a soft, baby blue.

After hearing the happy news, I browsed through my knitting album—the book that contains photos of every item I've knit. The memories unraveled like dropped stitches—that lacy, green blankie for our first grandchild. What joy each stitch gave me. The pattern was one of those with myriad rows that you can't memorize and have to pencil-in check marks to keep your place. No watching TV or talking to friends. As I knitted, I would daydream about other knitting I was working on—sweaters, hats, and mittens. Then my mind would drift to how I'd give the little one a bath, and how I hoped we'd be asked to babysit.

I never dreamed at the time what the blankies would mean to Larisa and Kristen, Jake and Teresa and little Toni—how they wouldn't sleep without them. And how many times I would hear, "Grammy, please fix this hole."

Other knitting grandmothers will understand: as soon as possible after our children announced their good news I would be off to my favorite yarn store, the Ladybug Knitting Shop on Cape Cod. There I would spend hours searching for the perfect pattern and selecting from the rainbow of colors that lined the walls.

I knew, after the first grandchild, to buy a little extra yarn to make a twelve-inch square in the same pattern. This was the convenient substitute for when the babies wanted to bring their blankies in the car or stroller, or for during the challenging time when the original, full-size blankie was in the wash.

Now, for number six, I knew which cuddly blue yarn I would use, but I needed to find the ideal pattern. I neglected chores to search through my files. It couldn't be feminine, of course, but it had to include some yarn-overs because I already knew how babies love to push their fingers through the holes when they rub the cuddly yarn under their noses.

I found the perfect pattern in an old Leisure Arts leaflet—a series of squares, each with five diagonal holes. The blocks were separated by little knit-one, purl-one-through-the-back-loop bumps. The pattern, appropriately named "Baby Blocks," was designed by Jean Lampe.

– – – –

The eighteen-row pattern wasn't intricate and I was able to memorize it easily, but it did require concentration. I inserted markers onto my twenty-nine-inch circular needle so I wouldn't work past a change as I daydreamed about the little argyle vest with matching socks I would make for baby Teddy as soon as he began to walk. The softest ever Dreambaby D.K. moved through my fingers as the blankie grew slowly. But I had plenty of time—five months to be exact.

Before a quarter of the coverlet was hanging from the needles, however, our daughter started having some trouble. By this time I was enough at ease with the pattern to go back to my weekly knitting meeting. What a wonderful support group these knitters were to me during the troubled times that followed.

Soon more tests revealed that Teddy would be a Down's syndrome baby. At first we were all devastated—the joy diluted with apprehension. What did that mean? We were aware of the Special Olympics, of course, and of what children with Down's syndrome could accomplish, but we did not know what our daughter and her husband could expect in day-to-day life, or what my husband and I could do to help without interfering.

On the Internet we found books to read, which we borrowed from the library. Although we normally don't take part in chat rooms, this seemed the right time, and we connected with other parents and grandparents of Down's syndrome children.

We were amazed and grateful for their words of encouragement. Dozens of families wrote what a joy this special child would bring into our lives. We knew it would be challenging, but we were looking forward to helping our children raise the sweet, loving person that every parent of a Down's syndrome child told us we could expect.

Throughout this time I was grateful for the hours I could continue working the baby blue yarn. I sat alone in my bedroom—no TV, no music, just the sound of the mocking birds in the trees outside my window. The repetitive motion calmed me and allowed a quiet time for personal prayer. At that time, it seemed our grandson would be a full-term baby, and I believed the snuggly blue blankie would be ready.

But then, unexpectedly, Teddy was born early by Caesarean section, with many problems. I hurriedly bound off the one-third completed coverlet, wrapped it in light blue tissue paper, and shipped it overnight delivery from our home in Cape Cod to California. Even though it was unfinished, Teddy was so tiny, it would wrap around him. I

- - - -

could always unravel the cast-off row and add to it later. Then my husband and I took the first available flight to be with our daughter and her husband, and to meet our new grandson.

But we were never to see him alive. On his fourth day, Teddy started his flight up to heaven. At the funeral, five aunts and uncles and his grandfather carried Teddy's coffin into the church—with his unfinished baby blue snuggly draped over the tiny white box.

Later, when we were alone with the bereaved parents in the mortuary, my husband and I wrapped Teddy's tiny body in the cuddly blue that had a barrel of love in every stitch. I placed his doll-like hands on top of the blanket with a finger through one hole and kissed him good-bye.

So now I imagine Teddy's up there with the all the other little angels having the fun he missed here on earth. Of course, everywhere he flies he carries his soft, cuddly, baby blue blankie, with his fingers pushed through the holes.

- - - -

Chapter 3

WORLDLY KNITS

"It was in Ireland during a wet November, a time when dampness seemed to camp out in my bones, that I learned to knit. It was a place where warmth didn't offer itself freely. In that climate, a hand-knit woolen sweater became, for me, a celebrated gift, a symbol of warmth, a garment that bucked me up and reminded me of the tenacity of life."

—Bernadette Murphy, Zen and the Art of Knitting, 2002

I sometimes think it would be fun to take one of those knitting-inspired vacations advertised in popular knitting magazines each year. To spend a week or two in Italy, Norway, Ireland, or Greece immersed in the traditional techniques and styles of knitting popular there, to shop for yarn in old-worldly shops, to catch a glimpse of a flock of sheep dotting a verdant hillside, would be luxurious—if only I could find the time. Until I do, the collection of essays in this chapter do a fine job of transporting me and my latest knitting project (a Norwegian sweater, no less) to some faraway lands, from the comfort of my very own easy chair.

Knitting is Work and the Widows of Sant'Arsenio

by Lela Nargi

Author Lela Nargi takes the reader to Sant'Arsenio, a small town in southern Italy, where women knit for the same reasons they did when the craft originated hundreds of years ago: because they must. Lela lives, writes, and knits in Brooklyn, New York. She is the author of *Knitting Lessons: Tales from the Knitting Path*, published by Putnam in 2003, and *Around the Table: Women on Food, Cooking, Nourishment, Love . . . and the Mothers Who Dished It Up for Them*, published by Tarcher in 2005.

The notion of knitting as hip has not dawned on the general populace of Sant'Arsenio, Italy. This town, in the southerly region of Campania, whose stone buildings contort down a jag of mountainside through olive groves and ancient chestnut trees toward the flat farmlands of the

Vallo di Diano, does, nevertheless, sit perched on the fringe of change. It's the same story as it ever was: youngsters balk at the tedious ways of their elders, dreaming of glamorous careers and of fast food instead of lives squandered on farming and household chores, and of everything new and flashy instead of anything old and traditional. On weekday mornings over at the convent, you can watch teenage girls in low-slung jeans, skimpy tank tops, and copious makeup slink to school while widowed octogenarians gawp in flagrant disapproval, as they stand in calf-length black skirts, stockings, and kerchiefs, sweeping their stoops.

Change has been slow to find a permanent toe-hold in Sant'Arsenio. Especially up the mountainside, where the oldest buildings and their occupants reside, it is easy to forget that anything at all exists, anywhere, of the new. Belled goats clang around in the undergrowth, foraging. Fig and apple trees drop their fruit onto narrow cobblestone sidewalks. In early October, the streets are clogged (comparatively) with farmers driving tractors or horse carts piled with fodder; the pungent smell of burning weeds wafts from the fields; in the arbors, the grapes are almost ripe for picking to make wine; and in the groves, netting has been spread under the trees to collect olives for pressing oil. Strike up a conversation with any one of these hardworking people and they will tell you that things are not what they once were around here, when everyone grew their own wheat to make flour, everyone made their own bread in wood-fired ovens, and everyone kept chickens, cows, pigs, and goats for eggs, milk, sausage-making, and cheese—and a fair number of women also kept sheep for wool they would spin into yarn.

"*La vita non é facile*," life is not easy, says Maria, who has just waddled down from the higher mountains carrying fifteen pounds of chestnuts, food for her pigs, wrapped in a tablecloth on top of her head. On which maxim one might circularly elaborate, upon further contemplation of the pace and manner of existence in this restless landscape:

1. Everything in the course of a minute, an hour, a lifetime, is work;

2. work always results in some material manifestation which is usually but not always practical, even as this work itself is

3. never ending.

It is evening and the widows are back on their stoops, sitting on makeshift chairs of crates topped with hand-sewn pillows. The work of the day has been wrestled into submission: gardens have been tended and fruit picked and houses cleaned and meals made and olive trees pruned and chickens fed and laundry hung out to dry and firewood tied into bundles and eggplant sliced and put to pickle in jars . . . and on and on. But as is the curse or blessing of people who know only work, the widows, assembled in small gossipy groups, do not take this obvious opportunity to rest.

Well, their bodies rest but their hands do not. Out come bags of cloth and thread and yarn, and the hooks and the needles. Maria busily cross-stitches a tablecloth with tiny flowers; stacked in a dresser in her parlor are dozens of table-cloths, bedcovers, and nightgowns, all intricately, mind-bogglingly embroidered, the work of forty years or more. Ask her about them and she will only reply with a shrug. (Everything is work, work always results in a material mani-festation, even as that work is neverending.)

Other women crochet lace curtains, bedspreads, and tablecloths, with fine white cotton thread; this work "deco-rates" their sparsely furnished houses. (The word decorate is used loosely here, as to decorate is to purposefully adorn something or someone rather than tossing a piece of cloth here or there because you need a place to put it and have run out of storage space in your armoire.) Still other women wield warped wooden knitting needles, some in the act of creating sweaters, scarves, or hats for certain young women who, though they would never dream of learning to knit themselves (hip? Hah!), recognize the benefit in style and fit of a handmade garment. It's just more work for the widows of Sant'Arsenio—and what they consider laughably profitable work; who in their right mind would pay for *knitting*?

Antonietta has fished out from her attic a small shopping bag that contains an assortment of knitting projects: several pairs of booties, three tiny hats, and a newborn's sweater. There hasn't been a baby in the family in four and a half years (Pier Francesco was the very last grandchild), and great-grandchildren are probably some years off (the oldest grandchild, Angelo, is only twenty-two years old and is still attending university). But Antonietta's fingers have to be busy with something while they wait for the morning's chores; and she has remembered that among the contents of this baby knitting bag is an unfinished blanket. The idea of a thing left undone is, frankly, unnerving. There is almost precisely enough yarn left to finish the blanket— Antonietta and the other widows of Sant'Arsenio are not prone to stashes since, of course, unused yarn means work to be done and when there is work to be done, you do it.

- - - -

In America, I tell Antonietta, knitting has become really hip; lots of young women, and even some men, have "discovered" it. She blinks at me flatly, the way she does when I don't know the Italian word for something and so make up one that is half French, half Spanish, and completely unintelligible. The breakdown in communication in this instance has less to do with the comprehension of a word than a way of life. That an activity could be "hip" implies that a person has leisure time in which to pursue it. But since for Antonietta and the widows of Sant'Arsenio everything in life is work, knitting is also work, and you do it because you must. Satisfaction, pleasure, perhaps even spiritual ease (although it is doubtful that Antonietta would ever describe it thus) come from the work itself, from its completion. And most importantly, from starting it again. And again.

NORSK KNITTING

by ERIC DREGNI

Having spent a year just south of the Arctic Circle in Trondheim, Norway, Eric Dregni witnessed firsthand the clever stitching of the Scandinavians. Dregni is the author of four books on motorscooters and recently indulged his obsession with oversized fiberglass statues in the book *Minnesota Marvels: Roadside Attractions in the Land of Lakes*. He's currently compiling his misadventures in Norway into a book entitled *Columbus Was Norwegian: and Other Things I Learned in Scandinavia*.

When our baby was born in Norway, distant Norwegian relatives gathered together to knit elaborate sweaters for the new little Viking. Just a month after hearing of the birth, a seventy-five-year-old woman named Ingeborg from the town of Bjørk sent us a thick sweater of the local Lusterfjord pattern with deep blues, ruddy reds, and some mustard yellows. We often heard the saying, "In Norway, babies are born with skis, the parents provide the poles." Apparently, the rest of the family knits the sweaters.

Besides *bunads* (the hand-embroidered folk costumes worn for formal occasions and country dances), the typical Norwegian outfit is a handknit sweater with matching hat, gloves, and knee-high socks, pulled up to where the wool knickers begin. Each region of Norway has a different style of sweater—similar to the different tartan patterns in Scotland. Bergen has the Fana pattern with stripes, Selbu invented the star and animal motif, and Voss has the classic yoked design.

Some Norwegians cringe at the quaint stereotype that they all run around in handmade sweaters and pass their time knitting. When my friend Astrid found out I was writing about Norway, she said, "That's great! Then you can dispel all the myths that Americans have of us that we go around in Norwegian sweaters and wear *bunads*." She soon confessed, however, to owning a *bunad* and a closet full of handknit sweaters. When winter came and almost all cross-country skiers wore this outfit, Astrid couldn't deny that it was the best outfit for skiing.

Other Norwegians want to preserve and honor this traditional craft of knitting intricate sweaters. A town named Selbu—outside of Trondheim, where we have been staying—

had a knitting circle of women famous throughout Norway because they developed their own patterns and were able to support themselves by knitting. In honor of these knitting revolutionaries, Selbu now boasts the Knitting Museum and Knitting Hall of Fame. Also, in the center of Trondheim, a military museum features mannequins of famous Norwegian resistance fighters during World War II wearing heavy Norwegian sweaters. Although the wool would keep them warm, the bright colors and patterns of these sweaters wouldn't offer much camouflage and probably made them easy targets for ruthless Nazis. Nevertheless, the Norwegian fighters certainly look festive and cozy in their beautiful sweaters, especially next to the drab storm troopers from Düsseldorf.

Norwegian children are indoctrinated into the world of knitting when they are young. In elementary school, children have knitting class to help with coordination, mathematics, and relaxation. The knitting propaganda on Norwegian youth even extends to jaded college students. I see some hip scholars riding the bus to class, clicking their knitting needles as their Walkman headphones blare Metallica into their eardrums.

Entrepreneurial Norwegians have translated this skill into a career. One woman sets up a stand in the center of

Trondheim to sell her homemade socks, gloves, and hats. (This is a common sight throughout Norway, especially around Christmas when the women vie for position on the busiest street corners.) That day, this woman sold me the most expensive pair of wool socks I've ever bought, but they're also the warmest.

Many older Norwegian women who ride the free "Meat Bus" to Sweden to buy cheap meat, knit during the entire two-hour trip. Norway has the highest prices in Europe, so even expensive Sweden is a relative bargain. The three-hour drive winds above the fjord into the snow-capped mountains and passes more moose-crossing signs than I can count. The driver, who steers the Meat Bus to Sweden every day, cracks jokes in funny voices and makes loud moose calls over the intercom. The women on the bus guffaw but never miss a stitch of their sweaters in progress. "Knitting helps pass the time and relaxes me," confesses one woman. During the bus ride, she finishes a pair of mittens for her grandchild, proving that knitting is not only a means to relax but a way to express her love.

She recommends knitting to my wife Katy as a way to unwind. Our baby is colicky, so we desperately need a way to calm our nerves after all the fussing. Katy decides to give knitting a try. In the center of Trondheim, she stops at one of the many knitting stores where women gather to knit complicated sweaters while they chat and drink strong coffee. I have high hopes that Katy's persistence will someday land her a coveted position in the Knitting Hall of Fame in Selbu. I envision the noble knitting council bestowing upon her the shining gilded knitting needles, and her handprint cemented in the future knitting walk of fame. My son and I will brag that we were there on that fateful day when she took up the needles and yarn to work her woolen magic.

To achieve this glory, Katy has to begin somewhere. The women at the knitting store show her some basic Norwegian sweater designs. "It's really very easy," they insist. Katy, who has never knit a stitch in her life, wisely chooses to begin with a simple one-color red scarf. Back home, she sets the Norwegian instruction book on her lap, casts on, and begins knitting and purling as the baby coos jealously alongside her. I keep the baby distracted, fed, and clothed with clean diapers while Katy tries desperately to relax with her new hobby.

In Katy's knitting book, full-color photos of luscious sweaters spur her on, and black-and-white line drawings attempt to explain each step of the way. Armed with her Norwegian-English dictionary, she deciphers the text but must set down her needles each time a new word stumps her. The loops slip off the needles, and some stitches are snug while others are loose. To even it out, she stops to stretch what little she has done, at which point the baby grabs the ball of yarn with his vice-like grip and pulls with all his might. The little scarf tightens up into a ball.

So much for relaxation. In a rage, Katy throws the yarn and needles across the room. The baby rolls over to them for a taste. Since the plastic needles are dull, we let him play with them to keep him quiet. When we notice his whole mouth and chin covered in red, we run to the rescue. Snatching away the knitting needles, we realize he's fine; he's just chewed up half of the red yarn; he cries when we don't let him keep eating.

Katy occasionally picks up the needles again, but the relaxation promised by her guidebook and by the woman on the bus never washes over her. After numerous false starts, broken thread, and unwound knitting (thanks to the baby's powerful grip), Katy has decided to hang up her knitting needles—at least until the baby is in college. With only two inches finished of her scarf, Katy's knitting career has come to an end. Perhaps as part of her master plan, however, she somehow convinces her friend Margaret to knit the entire red scarf for the baby.

– – – –

ANOTHER KNITTER
ON THE BLOCK

BY TEVA DURHAM

In "Another Knitter on the Block," author Teva Durham meets a knitter from the Brittany region of northern France in the worldly city of New York. Although it is knitting that brings the two women together, over time they become warm friends who connect on many different levels.

An avid knitter since the 1980s, when she was a restless youth, Teva (pronounced with soft "e") Durham founded loop-d-loop—an innovative line of hand-knits—in 2000. Her designs and articles are featured in *Weekend Knitting, Scarf Style, Knitting Lessons, For the Love of Knitting*, and multiple *Vogue Knitting* "On-the-Go" titles. Teva's first solo knitting book, *Loop-d-Loop: More Than 40 Novel Designs for Knitters*, was published by Stewart, Tabori & Chang in 2005.

Nestled amid the spires of midtown skyscrapers to the north, south, and east, and the racket and roar of the highway, Hudson River, and Donald Trump's endless construction projects to the west, my block seems to be the one that time forgot. It's an oasis in Hell's Kitchen. Once you pass the corner's grimy Blimpie sandwich joint, the tree-lined sidewalks widen. It always reminds me of a European city, especially with the clip-clop of horse and buggies en route to the stables after a tour of duty in Central Park. There are pre-war buildings with doormen and a cadre of whitewashed row houses, one of which I have lived in for the past fifteen years. The original idea was that if I was to bear keeping my "day job," I wanted to be able to roll out of bed and walk to Rockefeller Center, where said job was located. So for two months I spent lunch hours looking at vermin-infested walk-ups with dark, smelly hallways and rents that equaled three weeks' pay. Then, on the way back from another disappointing apartment, I happened across this stretch of 55th Street and fell in love. For two more months I hassled brokers for a listing on that block. And, after selling my step-grandma's ring to pay the fee, I got the lease to a tiny studio with all the aforementioned urban dwelling problems, but on such a quaint block that these could be overlooked.

This may seem a roundabout way of introducing my story, but in New York, real estate is like a seventh sense—space is at a premium and it informs our way of life. Then there is the sheer number of people, from all walks of life, who live in such close proximity but who each maintain separate little universes behind closed doors. Most New Yorkers I know peer into windows with keen curiosity tinged with greed. Catching glimpses of exposed brick or high ceilings, they wonder how far back an apartment sprawls and who lives there. I do this, but not with so much envy since I moved upstairs to the duplex apartment whose artist-worthy skylight I gazed at longingly for years. Still, the glow of a lamp behind a window on a cold night makes me ponder what the cozy occupant(s) is doing; so many windows flicker with the eerie light of TVs, and imagining all the people alone in the dark mesmerized by junk entertainment depresses me.

I spend every waking hour trying to get in as much knitting as I can. You could say knitting is my way of zoning out (usually to NPR, books-on-tape, or music). Well that was the protocol before I started my own business, had my daughter and got a book deal. I often wonder how my life would be now, if I hadn't got that foothold here in my twenties.

– – – –

My block is not filled with families. I think there are only three school-aged children, even though many of the buildings have larger apartments. For the most part there are singles, roommates, and childless couples. Situated on the edge of the theatre district, we have actors, dancers, musicians, and techies; I hear neighbors practicing scales and see sport jackets emblazoned with Broadway show logos, usually from the traveling company. This is a tough life that lends itself to being solitary. I know how it is. I went to a performing arts school. Even though my temperament is shy, I used to take all sorts of risks onstage, and I never felt more embraced and protected than when transforming myself into a character. But by the time I moved to my block, I had given up that dream. I had lived with an alcoholic actor/director for a few years and the ending had been very ugly. I felt washed up at twenty-five. I was lying low.

Soon after moving to this block, it became evident this is a "dog block." After a few years of witnessing what a social lubricant canines can be, I decided to adopt one myself. Having never before owned a dog, I was surprised at the security I felt walking in the city with all that loyal muscle and teeth at the end of a leash—especially since Cooper, my Border Collie–Lab mix, quickly grew to 90 pounds. I felt new freedom to walk and daydream (about mixing yarns, working out stitch patterns, short-rowing a collar) and not worry if I was being stalked.

I may appear to be at ease in public, but it takes all my energy to put on the persona and go outside. Cooper became my primary means of introduction to other residents on the block. Walking a dog is a step up from peering into windows, giving me a more discreet, closer glimpse into my neighbors' lives. There is a strange etiquette involved— letting the dogs sniff each other while making small talk and exchanging names (or not) with the owners. I have met many quiet, elderly men who long ago came from less cosmopolitan parts but who are too closeted for the raucous gaiety of the West Village and Chelsea. I have met women who you might call old maids, though maybe they were once married, maybe even had children. Now their loyal companions are Poodles or Pomeranians—and I can't blame them; I was finding Cooper a great comfort, personifying him, talking to him, and letting him sleep on my bed despite his shedding.

Most dog-owner conversation, if not limited to dog breeds and pet care, focused on the block itself. I learned new details about my building: the last few vacancies had been due to AIDS; in the 1920s the row houses had been annexed to create a rooming house for artists—each apartment originally had a dumbwaiter connected to a basement

- - - -

restaurant; in the 1970s the building had been an SRO (a single-room-occupancy welfare hotel); and older tenants are now being replaced by Yuppies.

One rainy fall day five years ago I was waiting for Cooper to "do his business" near the curb, when a woman, or rather, a knit coat, whisked past me. I didn't see her face, only a jaunty beret, and I watched the colorful fabric and the delightful silhouette recede as her spry steps took her to the corner where she turned. I had the urge to run and catch her and to ask where she'd bought that coat. Who designed it? Probably Missoni, but it also looked like Kaffe Fassett. Could she possibly have knit it herself? Did she live nearby or was she just visiting? A European tourist, I thought. Yet I had a vague recollection of having seen her and the coat before when I had been in a less observant mood.

A month later, a Yorkie owner who's on the Community Board urged me to come to the Block Association meeting. It was held in the meeting hall of the castle-like co-op building mid-block. I'd heard that in the 1970s Hari Krishnas had owned the building, and that pungent aromas of curry and incense and sounds of happy chanting wafted down the block. The renovated building's Romanesque interior was beautiful. There wasn't much of a turn out for the meeting, however.

– – – –

I slipped into one of the many metal folding chairs. As the officers at the card tables in front listed a number of items on the agenda—reelections, donations, Christmas lights, and caroling—I found myself studying the back of the woman seated directly in front of me. She was wearing an unusual Fair Isle sweater. It was made of a multitude of cotton and linen yarns in yellows, olives, and blues with the occasional jolt of lime, red, and orange. The gauge was about five stitches to the inch, and on closer observation I could make out that some colors were a single strand of yarn while others were several thinner yarns plied together. The pattern bands were very simple, short repeats over six rows or fewer—dots, hooks, triangles, checks. The sleeve colors did not match the shoulders, but harmonized with them. For me, looking at that sweater was like listening to Bach. The striped, ribbed neckband looked "picked up" and knit by hand. I couldn't see an indent at the back neck where a label would be sewn if this were a store-bought sweater. I had a sense about this woman, with her spry, thin frame, that she may be the woman in the wonderful knit coat, and in that case I may have found a master knitter on the block. Here was my opportunity. I eagerly awaited the wrap up of the meeting and hoped she was staying for the cookies and punch.

Now, I have to mention that by this time I had embarked on a career as a knit designer. Indeed, I had been an editor at the top pattern magazine and was attempting to launch my own line. This often made bonding with your "lay knitter" difficult. There is a type of knitting lady who is out to debunk every knitting upstart. I'd encountered many persnickety guild members and yarn shop owners whose aim is to trick you up if you're under forty. As soon as you mention your professional associations, they are skeptical. Nevertheless, I got up my nerve and approached this woman, who looked to be in her sixties. She had high cheekbones and translucent skin, piercing dark eyes, and grey hair that flopped into a kind of limp bob. Let's call her Elsa, for anonymity.

"I have to ask you," I began, "Did you knit that sweater?"

She replied with an accent. I later learned she grew up in Brittany, the Celtic part of France. I asked if she'd like to knit some samples for me for pay. She declined. She doesn't knit much anymore but almost every day she enjoys wearing what she's made. I explained how I'd seen the marvelous coat and that my mystery was now solved.

From that point on, whenever I'd cross paths with Elsa, it always seemed to be at just the right time. I'd say, "Stand back and let me take in your work of art. Have I seen this one before? I like how you put the green right there." And she would recall how that decision came about and from which shops the various yarns had come. I'd tell her about the projects I was working on and the progress in my career.

One time Elsa came up to my apartment and looked at my designs. She was afraid Cooper would jump up on her, so I tied him in the hallway. She explained that she had a colostomy bag and was afraid of the dog bursting it. She had mentioned once knitting a sweater for her radiologist's wife so I put two and two together. She said she often had to rush home when the bag got too full. She had an idea to start knitting again, if only to create a sweater with a kind of pocket into which the bag could fit. It could look like a belted purse and would match the sweater so well it would provide access and yet be discreet at the same time. She asked if I thought a magazine would publish such a design, as she hoped to make it available to other cancer survivors. I perfectly understood the way her creativity worked, even if this bodily function detail was a bit off-putting. But how many times had Elsa stood watching on the sidewalk while I scooped up Cooper's poop into a plastic bag?

We talked for hours in the excited way you do when you first click with someone. We discovered that we listened to some of the same wacky, radical radio shows on WBAI. She had worked for many years as a legal secretary for a boss who gave her plenty of time to travel. She told me that now she loved being alone in her own space with her books, whereas before it had been her knitting. Many of her friends had families and children with whom they spent holidays. But the trappings of marriage and bourgeois lifestyle were not desirable to her. She had no regrets (and she playfully sung the Edith Piaf song). She had become a Buddhist and she had decided not to have any more treatment.

One day when we met by chance, Elsa was glowing. She had just come from seeing the Dalai Lama in Central Park. Another day when we met, I was glowing. My lover had just dropped me off from the beach. I was in a sun-induced haze.

"I think he's married," I confessed.

I told her how he'd wanted to come live with me, but he'd never invited me into his apartment. When I demanded to know more about his living situation, he stopped asking to move in, even though we'd already bought furniture at IKEA together.

Elsa's eyes were like those of a good shrink—nonjudgmental and wise. I only once found a really good shrink,

- - - -

and by the time I warmed up to trusting her, I couldn't afford her anymore. I trusted Elsa's opinion right away, because she sought the same care and perfection in her knitting as I do; there are many avid knitters out there, but few who are able to express something deeper with their creative choices. I had felt an instant kinship with Elsa in this respect, and so I now looked to her for answers. I wanted to assuage my fear of being alone. Was being single only half a life? No, we agreed. In fact, by being single I wasn't *losing* part of my identity to become a unit in a relationship. Was I missing out on something? No, I agreed with her, I was only missing out on picking up his dirty socks.

Every summer, during the weekend of the Ninth Avenue Food Festival that halts cross-town traffic but brings droves of pedestrians, our block hosts an urban yard sale. Tenants are invited to set up stands on the sidewalk in front of their buildings—it's an opportunity to get rid of your brick-a-brack (and see all the junk your neighbors' apartments contain). That year I was surprised to find Elsa seated on a Persian prayer mat amid neat piles of hardcover books, whimsical pottery, and ethnic jewelry. She said she'd decided to clean house. Books were one dollar each and teapots, five dollars. Even though I had been on my way to a brunch or something, I found this opportunity hard to pass up. I first looked over the books. They were predominantly

- - - -

knitting books—some I owned myself, some not—along with eclectic subjects such as Jung, the Vikings, and Asian art.

"Are you sure you won't miss them?" I asked her.

Elsa said she had photocopied all the stuff she wanted and that she had more books to go through that would become available once she'd copied the relevant pages.

I ended up taking all twenty-nine books, plus three teapots: one in the shape of a little cottage, the second handpainted with bright blooms, and the third decorated with an Asian fish. We borrowed a trolley from her doorman and I wheeled the booty to my place.

On autumn nights, when I was at risk of being swallowed up by loneliness, when calls and voicemails to my lover went unanswered, I brewed pots of tea and worked into the wee hours. I would sometimes pause while pouring boiling water over fragrant leaves and draw comfort from thoughts of Elsa maybe having once done the same.

I called Elsa once, to see if she had more books she wanted to unload. She seemed groggy and distracted and at first confused me with someone else. It was an awkward communication. I wondered if her condition was deteriorating or if we just had a face-to-face relationship that didn't quite translate over the phone.

When I ran into Elsa the next spring, she seemed to be her same spry self. I had just been wondering if it would be worth calling her for advice. I was pregnant.

"I'm thirty-seven," I told Elsa, "I don't believe in messing with the hand of fate. I offered to marry him for the sake of the baby, but he said he had 'other plans.'"

I told her I was an emotional mess, but, by the way, my knitting kits were selling like hotcakes.

Could I be a good parent? My tendency was to hide, to burrow away and just churn out stitches, to live in a fantasy world of dreaming up garments to create little models of otherwise unobtainable perfection, with details only another enthusiast could appreciate. Now that I was starting a business, where did a child fit in? Maybe I was too self-absorbed, too preoccupied. I loved spending time with my nieces, but was always relieved to go home and not be stuck cleaning up the mess or getting them to settle down to bed. My family had little faith in my choices, except they were all too happy to accept Cooper as my significant other and surrogate child.

Elsa assured me that everything presents itself as a lesson we are ready to learn. And when I returned to my apartment, I recalled things Elsa had told me of her life, about her miserable childhood that involved step-sibling rivalry, about a sad long-distance love affair that lasted for years. I felt my belly where this strange new life was stretching the skin tight and giving me voracious hunger. And I thought of Elsa alone in her apartment down the block, dealing with her colon cancer.

I continued to bump into Elsa, now with my daughter in her Baby Bjorn carrier or in her stroller, with an aging Cooper alongside. Elsa and the baby would smile at each other.

"This is no ordinary girl," Elsa would say while pinching rolls of baby fat. "This is a Buddha!"

And she could tell from my smile how motherhood agreed with me. I felt more in-the-flow than ever. Actually producing a being from my body showed me anything was possible. It made me more present and engaged in daily life. My knitting was no longer something to hide behind or a buffer from the world but an active, outward expression of my creativity.

And then there was the time I found myself in Elsa's building, searching for my missing book-advance. There had been a mix-up with my publisher. I had waited and waited for my book-advance. Without a check in hand, it was hard to believe the contract had really gone through. It turned out that two weeks earlier the check had been FedExed to the wrong address.

"I think I know which building that is," I told my editor. "I'll go ask the doorman and call you back."

It was Elsa's building. I explained the mix-up to the

doorman and how desperate I was for the large check. He went to a big lock-up in the lobby and began to sort through packages.

"We keep most everything since we have so many sublets," he told me.

Just then, Elsa entered the lobby and I filled her in on the situation. She waited with me, and when the doorman produced the envelope, we jumped up and down and cheered as I ripped it open and kissed the check.

"I can't believe that you arrived to share this moment with me!" I exclaimed to Elsa.

When I got home, I called my editor with the news that I'd found the check. She told me I should go out and have a glass of wine with someone special to celebrate my book deal. My mind scanned through a list of friends who had become scarce since I'd become obsessed with knitting and even scarcer since I'd become a single mother; then I thought of my relatives. Sadly, I felt there was no one who could truly be happy for me without rivalry. Was this a failure on my part? Had I failed to bond? Maybe. But then there was Elsa, whose integrity I could really respect. "Actually," I told my editor. "I already celebrated." Part of me still longed to sit in a restaurant at the center of a lively thirty-something crowd. I had seen enough *Friends* episodes to envy the fictional tight-knit group, especially the unconditional love and support offered to Phoebe (the ditsy former street-kid with whom I most identified).

When I decided to write this piece, I had not bumped into Elsa for several weeks. I asked her doorman and he said, "Oh Elsa, what a special woman she is. We have been friends a long time. She has very interesting life in many countries. I was freedom fighter in Poland. And then I too had the cancer and she teach me many things. My dear, she is not doing so good. She doesn't go out no more and pretty much in bed now."

He said Elsa has a nurse's aid in every day. I am not sure what to do. I have the final galleys of my book, but it no longer seems so important to show her how well it came out. Maybe I feel ashamed of my good fortune or I really don't know how to be a friend. I wish I could offer to run errands for her, bring her soup and flowers, and make her more comfortable. But I'm not the type who charges in and takes care of people, and I worry about encroaching on her dignity and privacy. If I could muster the fortitude, I would ask her to entrust to me her sweaters so that I could document them and treasure them. Who could appreciate them more? Perhaps it is a selfish impulse to think about the sweaters, but maybe my plan would please her. I hesitate, wondering if I'm significant enough to her. Mostly, I am frightened to find out, and scared to face loss head on.

– – – –

Chapter 4

TO BE A KNITTER

"IT IS ALSO TRUE OF DEVOTED KNITTERS THAT THEY IM-
MEDIATELY FEEL A CONNECTION AND CAMARADERIE
WHEN MEETING A FELLOW KNITTER. THERE IS A SENSE
OF TRUST THAT OPENS A DOOR INTO CONVERSATION AND
OFTEN LEADS TO DEEP, LONG-LASTING FRIENDSHIPS."

—*Nancy J. Thomas and Ilana Rabinowitz,* A Passion for Knitting,
2002

As I sat hunched with intense concentration over the beginnings of a sleeve to a baby sweater, stitches barely clinging to the four size 1 double-point needles I held clumsily in my hands, I wondered about what it means to be a knitter. This was the third time I had tried to begin the sleeve, and I wasn't about to rest until I had a few rows on the needles and the stitches were secure. Were all knitters this determined, this crazy for their craft? In my experience, the answer is yes. Knitters also tend to be creative, motivated, and, well, somewhat compulsive. Many of the knitters I know have more yarn stocked away at home than they'll ever be able to knit in the next ten years. And they've got more than one unfinished object (affectionately known as UFOs) lurking in one or more dark corner of the house. If this sounds all too familiar, take heart. The essays collected in this chapter are proof that you're not alone.

HOW TO READ A PATTERN

BY LAURA BILLINGS

Knitting is definitely addictive. In her essay "How to Read a Pattern," writer Laura Billings finds it impossible to resist the lure of yarn, needles, and, most of all, pattern books . . . especially those filled with romantic images of forlorn-looking models dressed in tweed and wool. Laura is a columnist at the *St. Paul Pioneer Press* and is the mother of three boys, who don't actually like wearing anything she makes for them.

When the leadership ranks of both my knitting circle and my book group determined that we would henceforth be meeting on the third Thursday evening of the month, it became clear I was going to have to decide where my true loyalties lay.

The book club seemed the obvious choice. I'd been the group's founder, and I was the one who kept the mailing list, cleared my throat to call the meetings to order, and mediated a truce when the classics-only contingent threatened to kick out the chick-lit types. When I came to reflect on it, I realized that this group had been meeting for more than three years because of the sheer force of my will and in spite of new babies, overcrowded schedules, and growing antagonism about the work of Barbara Kingsolver. So I told the knitting circle I would miss their company, but duty called.

Judging by the book you hold in your hands, you can probably guess what happened. I went to the next meeting of my book club without that month's selection—which I'd never cracked—and a double-stranded felted mitten project I couldn't wait to finish. I apologized to the group and told them it wouldn't happen again, but it did, regularly. I recall one dark night, sitting in someone else's dining room, knitting by myself, and eating far more than my share of the book club's baked brie, and feeling just like the protagonist my friends were discussing in the living room, the one who realizes, too late, that he has married the wrong woman.

Fortunately, my book club and I had an amicable divorce.

That was more than three years ago, and I haven't looked back. True, I haven't finished a novel since then either, but I really can't blame the knitting. I have two boys under the age of three whose erratic nap schedules no longer allow me the long hours I used to spend stretched out on the sofa with a book. I find the few stitches I can accomplish between interruptions create the much-needed illusion of forward movement, whereas reading the same page forty-eight times just makes me mad.

My friends from the book club say they understand. But I can tell they worry that my brains have gone as soft as cashmere. What they don't understand—and what I've since discovered—is that knitting offers up its own world of literature, just as vivid and comforting, humane and richly detailed as anything on the *New York Times* bestseller lists.

I refer, of course, to pattern books.

The first one I ever bought was a collection of baby sweaters by the designer Debbie Bliss. Before then, I'd been a freeform knitter who made lumpy sweaters and scarves that never turned out as planned. Now pregnant for the first time, I suddenly wanted better for my kids. I taught myself the language of patterns by reading the glossary and trying to decipher between ssk's and psso's. Within a trimester or two, I had a few sweaters waiting for a child to wear them.

– – – –

But even after those projects were complete, I found myself turning to this book for more than just the directions. My nightstand at the time was piled high with books about childbirth, the care and feeding of newborns, baby name books—each one making me dizzier with anxiety that I wasn't getting my recommended dosage of folic acid and that whatever name we picked for him would be all wrong. The only book that offered any comfort was the baby sweater book. Flipping through it night after night, looking at photos of fat and happy babies in gorgeous and impractical cashmere sweaters assured me, as no other book could at the time, that everything would probably turn out just fine.

Naturally, I bought a few dozen more pattern books for precisely that reason. A collection had begun.

Nonknitting readers might argue that a pattern book is merely a catalog of projects, a wish book of what you'd make if you had all the time in the world and a hefty employee discount at your local yarn store. They may be nice to look at, even therapeutic, but they can't offer the same dramatic human narrative as a novel.

But that's the argument of a person who lacks imagination and craftiness—qualities knitters happen to have in spades. In fact, if you were to take a picture from your favorite pattern book, one that speaks to you for reasons beyond the loft of the mohair or the physics of the set-in sleeve, you will find you can easily stitch together the 1,000 words or so every picture is said to paint.

There's a book on my nightstand now called *A Season's Tale*, published a few years ago by the British knitting company Rowan. I was attracted to designer Kim Hargreaves's classically tweedy patterns, as well as to the book's intriguing cast of characters (those less starved for adult reading material might think of them as "sweater models") all set against the deep golds and tender purples of the Scottish glens.

I'm particularly taken with three of these characters—a white-haired man, a brown-eyed girl, and a woman with a far-away look and finely articulated cheekbones. I open the book again and again to the page this trio shares, only partly because I like what they're wearing. *What brings these people together?* I wonder, as I cast on and begin to spin my own yarn.

At first glance, you might mistake the older man for the younger woman's father. Many people have. But if you look closely at the giant turtleneck he is wearing, you will realize that no daughter could persuade her father to wear a sweater like that. He'd protest it was much too itchy, too trendy, too blue. The only sort of woman who could make a man of years wear something so age inappropriate would be a woman he loves—his much younger wife. The early scandal of their union—her mistrustful parents, his angry older daughter—have all mellowed into memory by the time this story starts. The little girl is their daughter, Georgina, named after his maternal grandmother, a wonderful knitter, by the way, who took care of him when he was orphaned as a boy.

In spite of their great love, good looks, and impressive real estate holdings in Scotland, this close-knit family may be unraveling at the edges. Why, for instance, is she sitting at the piano a few pages later, in a fabulous beaded mohair crewneck, looking so haunted and alone? Has she fallen in love with the rakish gardener on the following page, with his heavy-gauge sweaters and tartan kilt? Or is she the only one who knows of her handsome older husband's terminal prognosis?

I haven't worked it all out yet, but as you can see, it does help the time pass when you're working on a boring sleeve.

- - - -

As you might have guessed, my literary tastes run toward Henry James, Edith Wharton, Jane Austen, and E. M. Forster, which is why I have a few dozen Rowan books and magazines in my library. Their models are often shown accessorizing their lovely sweaters with floor-length tweed walking skirts, or mud-covered Wellington boots, as if consciously trying to evoke the spirit of Elizabeth Bennett or Isabel Archer. Often shot on location, a flip through a Rowan book always makes me feel like I've been somewhere, and can smell the curry cooking in the background, or the tang of the sea salt in the air.

And yet, there are pattern books for almost any literary mood. *Lord of the Rings* lovers and science fiction fantasists may find inspiration as far back as the druids in Alice Starmore's Celtic titles, or Elsebeth Lavold's Viking patterns, some of which seem just perfect for faeries and hobbits. Mystery readers, who like to gather up the hidden threads, might turn to Kaffe Fassett's complicated colorwork, which may be strewn with hidden clues. Environmental types might be drawn to Sasha Kagan's leaf patterns. Dramaturgs who can't get enough Ibsen and Chekhov will warm up to the icy northern European beauties in the Icelandic Lopi booklets. And when I'm in the mood for something Bridget Jones-y, there are a half-dozen chunky-yarn pattern books to appeal to the knitting renaissance of twenty-somethings, which generally feature a simple pattern for covering a cell phone or a package of condoms. There's something for everyone.

And if you learn to read a pattern like I have, you will see that you don't really have to choose between having a life of the mind, or a sweater you can actually finish. You can have it both ways.

This brings me back to the book club, which has lately decided to switch their meetings from Thursday to Wednesday, which means I've been invited back in the fold. Having lately regained some of my lost reading time, I have to admit I'm eager to be reacquainted with books that do not all begin with two inches of k2p2 ribbing. Even so, I'm grateful to my pattern books for the do-it-yourself skills they helped me develop during my motherhood-imposed reading hiatus.

When I need a comforting yarn, I now know how to spin one myself.

– – – –

ODE TO MY STASH

BY SIGRID ARNOTT

Who can resist the occasional urge to buy a soft skein of wool in the perfect shade of gold, periwinkle, or sage green? In her essay "Ode to My Stash," writer Sigrid Arnott asks, "Why try?" Sigrid lives in Minneapolis. She recently transformed her husband's messy sock drawer into his own, personal yarn stash, so he wouldn't feel left out. Her sons won't knit but they like making yarn webs for Spider-Man.

For a long time I wouldn't admit to having a yarn stash. The word "stash" sounded like something shamefully hoarded so as not to have to share—or to avoid detection. Mine was not some dirty little secret stowed away in a sock drawer, nor a filled-to-bursting closet, just a few innocent skeins of yarn stored here and there.

I even found reasons to look down on yarn stashers. First of all, I thought, isn't knitting supposed to be all about, well, *knitting*, not storing? Yarn stores can do that with their shelves and drawers and storage space. After all, most of us don't live in mansions with a library, billards room, and yarn safe, so why clog up precious closet space with woolly stuff? Also, I thought it silly to spend money on something you *might never use*. Stashers I knew cheerfully spoke of yarn they had bought for complex sweaters they might not have the patience to actually undertake, or for that special shade of turquoise that they couldn't actually wear. I thought the prudent knitter should decide on a reasonable project, then buy the yarn when they had the time to undertake it.

No, I didn't have a stash—or so I thought.

I did give a home to orphaned yarn when some grandmas went to needlework Valhalla, then I had a few balls left over from projects, and a knitting basket. . . . That could hardly be considered a "stash," I figured.

Then one day my husband and I did an attic-to-basement house-tidying of our elderly bungalow. Normally we wouldn't dream of such a grand undertaking, but we were having the value of our house appraised. We naively figured that for every corner and closet of our compact home that looked spacious and open, our house might be higher valued. As we cleaned, trying to imagine how our house might look through the eyes of a real estate appraiser, little fiber caches came to my attention in almost every room. Only the kitchen and bathroom were fiber-free—that's where I tend to peruse those mail-order catalogs with covers of suggestively posed hanks of seductive yarns.

In the attic there was a box of Norwegian sport-weight yarn; in my bedroom a drawer of the same, a few plastic bags, and an old suitcase stuffed full of odds and ends. This suitcase, a mock-leather Samsonite, once belonged to my grandmum, the knitting queen of the family, and in it I had put what was left from her stash. Later, I rescued my husband's grandmother's yarn and needles from the Goodwill pile when the family was going through her personal effects, and also placed them in the suitcase. The suitcase represents the genesis of my yarn collection as well as my knitting ancestry. The grandmas, who never met, have been united in yarnland.

There were also ziplock bags filled with yarn my son and I dyed with Kool-Aid, and swatches for sweaters too ugly to pursue. I must admit to a couple UFOs as well, two sleeves of sweaters with complex colorwork—the kind of knitting that requires the attention a mother of youngsters can rarely give.

In the living room, a basket and knitting bag were tucked into corners, and in the dining room I found handwound balls decoratively displayed on the sideboard like some inedible, yet appealing cornucopia (I *do* change the arrangement at least seasonally). Next to my desk I have shoved the books to the back of the cases to make room for chromatically organized piles of yarn—blues on one shelf, yellows the next, even a group of the rare oranges. A basket on the piano was attractively filled with plump skeins in pastels like a flower bouquet. I began to wonder what the average person must think of my idea of interior decoration.

And then I began to wonder about myself. Did I have a problem?

This was the first time I had actually viewed all of my yarn within a twenty-four-hour period, and it was a little scary. It's true, I didn't have yarn hidden under floorboards or a closet stuffed with overflowing skeins, but a whole series of caches had infiltrated my house. Some of it was secreted away (that suitcase, for example) but much of it was on display—as if its obviousness could conceal evidence of outright hoarding.

I had to admit it: I had a stash.

It was like a fungus I once read about. Scientists had discovered that a certain type of mushroom that popped up over a hundred-square-mile area was all part of a single living, interconnected organism. Viewed individually, my ever-changing wool bouquets had seemed aesthetically pleasing and harmless. Now, looked at as a whole, it was clear that a fiber force-field was extending itself into the very matrix of my home. And I was responsible for its propagation.

- - - -

Why had I created what I had so often looked down upon?

Typically, a stash is made to insure against a time of future scarcity. For example, squirrels stash nuts under my perennials before winter's scarcity, and some males of our species have been known to stash boxes of cereal behind the couch in the living room for times when food is scarce. My parents were both children of the Depression and we lived on a Montana ranch twenty miles from a grocery store, so I grew up thinking that large stashes of food were normal and necessary. If we were low on bread, for example, we could look in freezer #2 (freezer #1 had a steer in it). We children were oftentimes enlisted to push overladen shopping carts so canned goods could be bought by the case. While my college friends came back from holiday vacations with some new clothes, I was often loaded down with some new clothes and pounds of canned pork and beans or creamed corn. Yes, these stashes were good to have.

But, really, with six or seven local yarn stores within a five-mile radius, mail-order catalogs galore, and the Internet, it's hard to imagine a time when I might be unable to procure yarn. Do I imagine scenarios where yarn might be a scarce commodity? I must admit I amuse myself with fantasies that discontinued Alice Starmore yarns will someday be worth more than money invested in IBM, or that I have to clothe my entire family (of men!) with eyelash novelty yarns from my stash. But these fantasies have nothing to do with my behavior; fear of scarcity does not propel me to sheep festivals. The only anxiety I harbor is the not-so-outlandish fear that my favorite colors of my favorite yarns will be discontinued. After all, it happened before when Tapestry in Goblin Green disappeared from the face of the yarn universe. (Note to yarn companies: Are you considering "reissues" of yarn classics?)

Could my behavior be genetically encoded? Some of my recent ancestors also seemed prone to another kind of stashing best summed up by their explanations, "It might come in useful someday." My father was an engineer and an inventor as well as a rancher and welder. He was also Scotch, and hated senseless spending and waste. So he would take ancient, worn-out machinery, cut it up, add some hydraulics, and weld it into some new hybrid farm-implement. To do this you basically need your own personal scrap yard—a machinery stash. He must have had plans for his hot-water-heater stash and all the kitchen ranges stowed in the machine shed, too, but they were never realized.

It sometimes seems that some primeval urge dictates that I acquire yarn—yarn that I will *need* for some future, yet-to-be-imagined project. Like some distant ancestor who obsessively plucked wool from thorns to later spin and clothe

– – – –

her family, or my dad who snatched stoves from potential scrap heaps, I often pace the aisles of yarn stores searching for the "perfect yarn," or I snatch up thrift-store skeins without calculating my remaining storage space.

I also admit to a simple love of fiber. Fabric is nice, but for me nothing can beat the primal attraction I feel toward a skein of wool. Looking at the other women rapturously stroking their purchases as they pile them on the yarn-store counter, or pausing in awe before a rainbow display of skeins, they too appear to be motivated by desire rather than disaster-preparedness precaution. I anticipate getting that yarn home (maybe sneaking it into the house) to be played with, stroked, swatched, gloated over.

Like the giant fungus that was much greater than just a few toadstools under a tree, my yarn bouquets manifest something more complex than just a pile of yarn somewhere. My stash is not so much a place (a closet or a trunk) as a symbol of my knitting mentality. Mixed in with a nostalgia for my knitting grandmum and my admitted fiber desire, is a need for ready access to yarns of all colors and qualities that really do "come in useful" to realize my textile creations. Sometimes my stash does come in handy in an emergency. It happened quite recently when I discovered that the yarn I had hoped to knit for stress-reduction during a long flight had an odd odor that made me feel, well . . . anxious. My stash was there to provide a substitute.

Most frequently, however, the web of yarn growing in my house has a more basic function. Maybe I'm having one of those days when I feel deprived, lonely, or inadequate. I open a drawer full of plump skeins neatly arranged by chroma, and run my hands over the bouncy fibers. I pull out a deep maroon and lively green, imagining a pair of fantastic mittens—suddenly I feel like the luckiest girl on the block, queen of all that I see in the drawer and through my inner eye.

After the shock of admitting that I really had a stash, I guiltily considered drastic means of "stash reduction" (and I'm not talking about knitting). Maybe there was a self-help program for women who buy too much yarn and can't knit fast enough to use it up, or a program to follow for yarn fasting. Then I considered the valuable gifts my harmless pleasure gives me.

Like Uncle Scrooge, the Disney duck who frequented his vault just to revel in piles of gold and bathe himself in a shower of coins, I sometimes need to plunge myself into the abundance of a yarn basket or two. But unlike the miser who only wants to hoard, I promise my skeins that I will someday liberate them from my stash, transformed into some beautiful, knitted garment.

– – – –

REALLY, IT'S NOT SO BAD
or DERMATITIS OF THE LAMBS

BY AMY R. SINGER

Most yarn addicts can't imagine having an allergy to wool. Why, that eliminates half the yarns a knitter has to choose from, right? In the following essay, writer Amy Singer finds a way to continue knitting prolifically *and* avoid the wool that makes her itch. Amy is the editor of Knitty.com, a web-based knitting magazine with a sense of humor and absolutely no doily patterns. Her first book, *Knit Wit*, was published in 2004. She lives in Toronto with her husband Philip and their daughter, a mini-rex rabbit named Newton, who grunts in her sleep.

It always comes up in conversation. I don't *mean* to talk about it. But when knitters get together, it's inevitable. "Oh, I'd love to do [whatever wool-based knitting thing we're talking about], but I'm allergic to wool." You should see the wide-eyed looks people give me, oozing with pity and sympathy. It's like part of me just fell off in front of them.

Sure, I get why. I shop at the same yarn stores the wool junkies do. I know what I'm missing.

I know that wool captures the light differently than the yarns I can use; in fact, I can usually spot a yarn's fiber content from twenty paces without even reading the label. I've stared longingly at the wall of Zara at the big shop downtown, each ball so softly, perfectly spun, in every possible color. I've seen the hand-dyed handspuns that people bring home from Rhinebeck by the trunkload. I know about the South American co-ops where women apply ancient alchemy to fresh fiber, dyeing softly twisted skeins in kettles. I see the gleaming piles of hand-painted roving for sale at fiber festivals, practically free, for heaven's sake. Oh, and "wool is easier to spin than other fibers, you know."

Shut up. I know. Trust me, I've heard it all. I can't touch the stuff. Must you rub my nose in it?

Okay, it's time for an aside. At about this point in any "I'm allergic to wool" conversation, some well-meaning amateur physician—friend, knitter, yarn-shop salesperson—will offer their explanation for my trouble:

It's the dye. [No.]

It's the chemicals they use to process the stuff in. [Negatory, although they probably don't help any.]

It's the fiber itself. I've had the nasty needle-prick test from my allergy doctor and it's conclusive: Amy is allergic to wool.

Are you wondering what it feels like? If you promise not to get all doe-eyed, I'll tell you. When I pick up a particularly troublesome skein, within a few seconds, my hands start to feel like they're on fire. If I wash them thoroughly with a mild soap, the feeling eventually subsides. Some yarns, like superfine merino, or other animal fibers, like baby alpaca or kid mohair, I can tolerate—even work with—for a short while. But eventually, my hands start to feel like I've been rubbing them on fine sandpaper. They get super tender and hypersensitive. It's not a nice feeling.

You're probably wondering if I'm some sort of knitter-in-the-bubble freak of science, allergic to everything. No. Just this. Okay, I also get a similar reaction to cedar trees and tomato plants, but since I don't knit much foliage, it hasn't been a problem.

Many years ago, to be certain my doctor wasn't full of crap, I tried an experiment. I bought enough yarn to make a hat for a friend. Red Pingofrance, 75 percent acrylic and

- - - -

25 percent wool. That's almost no wool at all, really! What could happen? Certainly I wouldn't die. I started knitting. My hands soon felt like they were burning, but as an experienced obsessive, I decided this was probably in my head and just kept working. By the third day, as I wove in the last end of the now-hated ribbed cap, I retreated to my bed, thoroughly defeated, with a horrible cold.

Convinced? Me too.

So that's the bad part of it. And it *is* a real pain. I know how great that untouchable stuff is. I see what my friends and other knitters can do. Don't even mention felting. I ache to felt.

Except that this allergy is not all bad.

In fact, like any adversity that doesn't kill you—and as adversity goes, this one's pretty trivial—it makes you reach out for alternatives. I wasn't going to stop knitting just because most handspun and the majority of commercial yarns are off-limits to me. I could get creative, or I could take up scrapbooking.

I got creative.

I started touching every nonanimal thing I could find in every yarn store I visited and buying an occasional prospect to test. I have a boxful of one-ball wonders [also known as experiments not worth continuing], and as a result, I am getting quite good at knowing what to actually buy and what's not worth my money or time. I've also had many long-held assumptions completely destroyed by my years of informal research. I share the anecdotal results with you now.

ASSUMPTION ONE: COTTON YARN = BUTCHER'S TWINE
This is and isn't true. When I first claimed knitting as my craft of choice, it was the 1980s. Cotton was mostly stringlike, with no give and little softness. Things I knit from it grew with each wearing and only a severe hot-water wash and high-temp dry could return the knitted thing to its original shape. Sort of. Damned depressing to carefully cable a pretty vest only to have it turn into a knee-length tunic within hours of putting it on. Some of that nasty, heavy, stringlike yarn can still be found for sale today. I cannot explain this.

Pingouin [RIP] figured out that blending cotton with synthetics, like acrylic, made it softer. The yarn still didn't have as much stretch as their wool yarns, but it also didn't sag as a result of its own weight anywhere near as badly as 100 percent cotton.

At some point in the 1990s, other yarn companies started innovating. Even pure cotton, when spun into yarn just the right way or woven into little knittable tubes, is now being made soft. Have you touched the organic cottons? Soft like a baby's tushy, with a bonus: environmental friendliness. There are so many different types of cotton yarn available now that I could never knit them all. But I'm working on it.

I've also learned that, for me, some cottons—no matter how pretty—just aren't worth the tsuris. Mercerized multistranded cottons shimmer like silk. It takes a strong will for me to resist their gleam. But since they also split like mad and leave fine, shimmery thread loops all over my work that hide from notice until I've bound off, I avoid them.

Assumption two: synthetics suck

Okay, go back to the 1980s and yes, synthetics sucked. But that was the era of Phentex—frothy plastic filaments masquerading as yarn. Ever since some clever person figured out that you can turn used plastic soda-bottles into warm, soft, breathable fleece, we wool-free knitters have started to see similar improvements in synthetic fiber yarns. Synthetics can be suck-free!

Most importantly, synthetics can add durability, shimmer, and texture. And my favorite—stretch. Blend anything with Lycra and I'll try it once.

– – – –

Assumption three: cotton and blends are only good for spring and summer knitting

Twice a year—spring and fall—yarn companies introduce new yarns, colors, blends, and fibers. I get really excited when the new spring-summer lines come out, because that's when I'll find new cottons and cotton-blends to work with.

I'm not sure why most yarn companies think you can't knit fall-winter stuff in cotton, cause you absolutely can. All my handknit cotton winter hats are warm and machine washable. Almost every one of my recently knit cotton [and blend] sweaters was meant for winter wear and trust me, they're more than warm enough.

But I also know this: yarn companies can discontinue new cottony yarns almost as quickly as they introduce them. Some lines don't last past a season. So when I see something I like and it knits and washes well, I STOCK UP.

Assumption four: nothing else can possibly do the work of wool

Ha! Wrong! Wool snobs, I understand your passion. But you must accept that your fiber of choice is not the only one worth using. Clearly it can take a lot of fiddling to find a wool-free yarn that has the required properties for the project at hand, but it can be done.

For example, everyone I knew was knitting a Charlotte's

Web lace shawl in delicious Koigu two-ply merino and I couldn't . . . but I wanted to. So I went searching for an alternative that would show off the lace pattern and be as beautiful as the original. With more than a little desperate optimism, I experimented with a gorgeous 500-yard skein of pure two-ply Fleece Artist silk. It turned out to be such a good choice, and so surprisingly affordable, that other wool-snob knitters who have seen my finished shimmery silk shawl are knitting one like it.

Not only have I knit two of these silk shawls, but as a result of this $60 experiment, I discovered a love for a fiber I had thought was beyond my yarn budget [it's not, if I choose wisely] and hard to handle [again, no. In fact, you'd be surprised at how well the two-ply silk took the blocking. A thorough pinning and spritzing and poof—perfect lace that has stayed put through multiple wearings].

I wouldn't, however, knit an Aran in two-ply silk—my experimentation does not extend into intentional stupidity. Thankfully, there are light, stretchy cotton-blends that can do cables and texture gorgeously. And when it comes to socks, the only thing I use is a cotton-Lycra blend that holds its shape and is machine washable. It means I have a finite color palette to choose from, but at least I can knit socks too!

ASSUMPTION FIVE: AS YOU ARE, SO WILL YOU ALWAYS BE

Um, no. That's not true. In the last year, I've met quite a few people who *used* to be allergic to wool. One cured herself with a religiously applied course of homeopathic medicine. I was ready to find myself a homeopathic doc and get started until I heard the kicker—she had to give up coffee as part of the cure. Never mind.

Another knitter I know just grew out of her wool allergy, she told me.

Me? I did the weekly allergy shot thing for more than a year when I was a child, with no discernable improvement. A retest when I was in my twenties showed I was still allergic. So when it comes to needles, I think I'll just avoid hypodermics and stick to circulars.

WHY MY KNITTING WORLD IS A VERY HAPPY ONE

In the 1980s, not so much. But now? Now I'm ecstatic. New yarn shops are opening everywhere. Knitting is on TV. New knitting books are featured right up front in bookstores all over the continent. Knitwear is on the runways, in stores, around every neck in town. And there have never been so many yummy wool-free yarns for me to work with.

– – – –

So don't pity me. Instead imagine me diving into my stash of cloud-soft organic cotton, gleaming spun silk, wacked-out Japanese plant fibers, and hand-dyed flora of every description.

It may not be as easy to be a wool-free knitter, but my knitting is just as much fun as yours, and I'm never even a little bit itchy.

- - - -

Curse the Fruit Hat

by Amy Nelson Sander

Amy Nelson Sander started her first knitting club in 2000 with grand expectations that turned to myriad frustrations. When she's not squinting at a pattern or trying to correct a dropped stitch, she spends her time as an editor at the *St. Paul Pioneer Press* and as a teacher of aspiring journalists at the University of Minnesota. She also enjoys chasing around her two active children . . . on most days, anyway.

I once had this great idea to start a knitting club, until the whole thing started to unravel on me. I was a new mom, just heading back to full-time work and feeling slightly more domestic than my nondomestic self (it must have been the hormones from childbirth). Knitting was all the rage at the time—big-time stars like Gwyneth Paltrow and Madonna were featured in magazines knitting and purling between movie takes—and our friends were showering us with adorable homemade gifts like sweaters and booties, blankets and bonnets. Never mind that I had never put two needles together, didn't knew what a skein is, and didn't know how to wash the yarn: Before baby, I had never changed a diaper, didn't know what myconium is, and didn't know how to wash a newborn, and still I was handling motherhood sufficiently.

The knitting club started innocently enough. I suggested the idea to a friend, also a new mom, who actually knew how to knit. I was looking at the endeavor more as a way to gather monthly with other smart women, discuss issues, and eat fattening desserts—a mom's day out, if you will. If scarves got made and mittens were knit in the process, all the better.

We started by inviting friends and picking out supplies. Most of the other women who joined us were new to knitting as well. At the first few gatherings, my experienced knitter friend patiently taught us the basics and we paged through the exciting and colorful books of patterns she brought along.

The designs all looked pretty complicated to me, but I figured that if I could follow a recipe and make somewhat edible lasagna, I could follow a pattern and turn out something wearable. Maybe I should start with a scarf, I thought—no, maybe not so ambitious. Maybe a potholder.

How hard could a potholder be? Maybe a beer coaster. That seemed more my style. Then I came across what would become my nemesis: the Ann Norling kid's fruit-hat pattern. You know the one—it's red, looks like a strawberry, and tapers into a stemlike top. I *loved* the fruit hat. I loved how you could use red and green for the strawberry motif or pick up purple and black to make an oddly shaped eggplant or really live a little and go with blue and darker blue for a daring little blueberry. I would make the fruit hat and it would be my first knitting success of many, I decided that day.

I picked out all of the supplies for the project—bamboo needles, cotton-blend yarn, a set of double-point needles, and, of course, the fruit-hat pattern. I felt inspired, or, at the very least, motivated. I had a pattern and I had a purpose, but first I needed to master the fundamentals of casting on and keeping track of my stitches. Holding the needles felt awkward at first. I was used to holding pens and markers in my hands, but that was about it. The yarn was slippery and kept inching off the end of the needle. If knitting was supposed to be so relaxing, I wondered why my fingers were so tense and achy after our afternoon gatherings.

After our third or fourth gathering, the other knitting clubbers were starting to get the hang of what they were doing—one woman went home and, with her husband, worked out the algebraic formula for the most efficient way to knit; another just skipped all the beginners projects and plunged into an advanced sweater that turned out gorgeous; a third made a baby blanket as fine as lace—one I'd frame and put on a wall before I let any child spit up on it—while I was still stuck trying to get my fingers to do what I was willing them to do, still working on getting the right gauge so I could eventually start the fruit-hat pattern.

I *longed* to start the fruit hat. I pictured it already finished and placed jauntily atop the head of my stubborn child who refused to wear hats. I skipped ahead to the vision of me knocking off three more fruit hats before the holidays, to send as gifts to young relatives. I longed to start the hat, but for some reason I let a little bit of fear of failure and a whole lot of excuses delay me until I felt really ready.

And delay I did. Our monthly gathering now is well into its fourth year—more than enough time for any beginner to become an advanced knitter. Many of my friends who were at the original gathering have completed incredible projects. When we meet, my fellow knitters are kind and encouraging and inquisitive. Our gatherings usually start with us explaining what we are working on, what kind of yarn we are using, and where we got the pattern or idea. We share tips, like knitting websites; we share supplies, like needles and scissors; and we share stories, like about the quirky personality of the aunt for whom one friend is knitting mittens or how the baby sweater likely won't fit the baby by the time it is actually finished. And we share laughs, like the running joke about me still working on the same scarf from months earlier.

Our fluid group has seen some friends drop out, move on, or move abroad. All but one member have been pregnant at least once during that time, and many of us are on our second child now—more and more chances for me to make that fruit hat for one of the many baby showers and christenings. Invitations to the showers, first birthdays, and baptisms seemed to only heighten my frustration at not having finished the fruit hat. A cute little baby hat would have been the perfect gift for any of these occasions.

I think that may be where my unraveling started. I seemed to be all wrapped up in how everyone else was succeeding on their knitting projects and was feeling a little

- - - -

too sorry for myself about not completing one small cap. Nobody chided me or challenged me or judged my lack of initiative. Not that they would or should have. The core group of knitters in my club has known me since college, and they knew I likely wouldn't start something unless I thought I could finish it.

It's not that I'm a perfectionist—far from it, in fact. I look around the house now and it's filled with mementos of my good intentions gone by the wayside. There's the electric guitar for which I never started lessons; the yoga video still in its cellophane wrapper; the application for a mid-career study abroad that's only half filled-out and is past its expiration date. And it's not that I won't start something unless I think I can excel at it—my personal mantra is "pretty good still has the qualifier 'pretty' in it, now doesn't it?"

I even had inspiration from some people around me who were trying new things without being the best at them. I'm so proud of my forty-year-old friend who just completed private swim lessons to help her conquer her fear of the water, and proud of a different friend who took up running after years off, training for and finishing her first marathon. And then there was my husband, who, having never been on hockey skates before in his life, decided at age thirty he wanted to play hockey and joined an adult beginner league. He says he was (and still is) pretty awful, but he loves the game nonetheless.

But something was still holding me back from starting that fruit hat. That albatross around my neck. That white elephant. That darn cute little stem on that strawberry. Was it inertia, ineptitude, or inexperience? Maybe a combination of all three.

I came to the point where I *cursed* the fruit hat. I resented the spark of excitement it initially ignited and all of the not-enough-time, if-only-I-could-focus failures and half-starts it represented. I was surprised by how jealous I was of everyone else in the group who seemingly had no problems learning a new skill with ease. Or of finding the time to finish their projects. Or of having no qualms about ripping out rows and rows of stitches if they noticed an error halfway through their project. I was starting to think the only thing I was really good at was starting groups and watching others flourish.

Then something wonderful happened. I got secret word from my coworker that she was pregnant with twins after she had longed for children for years. There's not much more inspiring news than that. She wasn't a member of my knitting club; in fact, she probably didn't even know I had struggled with the skill about as long as she had struggled to have a child.

With her baby shower approaching, I decided I was going to knit fruit hats for her twins if it killed me. I gained confidence and set aside my self-pity. It finally was the time for me to do this. I had nothing to lose; in fact, nobody needed to know if I didn't accomplish my goal. But, in less than two weeks, I finished two fruit hats! I was bleary-eyed, my hands hurt, and one of the hats was significantly smaller than the other—but I did it. My knitting club would have been so proud of me.

I wrapped up the hats on the day of the shower and beamed when the mother-to-be opened the gift. Another coworker clucked, "Wow. Mother, wife, full-time employee, *and* knitter. Is there anything you can't do?" Oh, if she only knew. I have to admit, I so *love* that fruit hat.

Chapter 5

THE ZEN OF KNITTING

"KNITTERS WHO'VE BEEN AT IT A WHILE EXPERIENCE A TRANCELIKE STATE THAT PROVIDES THE SAME BENEFITS AS OTHER FORMS OF MEDITATION. UNLIKE OTHER FORMS OF MEDITATION, THOUGH, WHEN ALL IS SAID AND DONE, KNITTING PRODUCES A BEAUTIFUL, HANDCRAFTED, WEARABLE WORK OF ART. EACH GARMENT REFLECTS ITS UNIQUE MOMENT IN TIME AND IS AS SINGULAR IN ITS CONSTRUCTION AS THE PERSON WHO KNIT IT—AN IMAGE OF ITS CREATOR'S SPIRIT."

—*Bernadette Murphy,* Zen and the Art of Knitting, *2002*

Many knitters swear by the meditative quality of knitting. There's something about the feel of the soft yarn gliding across fingertips and the repetitive motion of knitting a stitch and slipping it off the end of the needle that soothes and calms an anxious mind. Worries seem to disappear and the mind is free to drift. The act of knitting provides a sense of purpose and direction during those times when everything else seems out of your control. In each of the essays featured in this chapter, knitting provides comfort when it is needed most.

WOOL AND REMEMBRANCE

BY MARGRET ALDRICH

Knitting soothes writer Margret Aldrich when she learns her father has leukemia, and it brings back fond memories of helping her father shear sheep one March afternoon on her family's sheep farm. Margret and her husband live in Princeton, New Jersey, where she is the intellectual property associate at Princeton University Press. She also works as a freelance writer and is the editor of two anthologies, *This Old Quilt* and *Once Upon a Quilt*, and the coeditor of *This Old Guitar*, all published by Voyageur Press.

There are certain things in this world that can spark a flood of memories. For some, a particular song might bring to mind their senior prom and the boy who broke their heart. For others, a smell can evoke a childhood memory of their great-grandmother's kitchen. For me, knitting and the feel of wool under my fingertips makes me think of my father and one bright March afternoon on our family's Midwestern sheep farm.

The members of my immediate family have notoriously bad memories. The memories themselves aren't bad, for the most part, but our ability to recall them is. While seemingly useless tidbits stick in our heads, pieces of vital information are often irretrievable. My mother, for example, might forget why she went to the grocery store, but she has an uncanny ability to conjure up detailed descriptions of what she was wearing at any given moment of her lifetime. My father acknowledges his lack of memories with pride, as if dwelling on what has already occurred is simply impractical, but I suspect that he could regurgitate the plotline of any given *Andy Griffith Show* on cue. My sister has virtually no memory at all, the poor thing. She has no sense of smell either, and I've long suspected that this disability is the result of simply forgetting how to use it.

Admittedly, my own memory is selective. I tend to recollect only certain vivid scenes from my years growing up in the seventies and eighties on the corn-covered plains of Iowa, and the details that elude me are a never-ending source of frustration. No matter how many times I ask, I can't commit to memory the year my family's farmhouse was built or what kind of wood was used to construct the heavy beams that crisscross its ceilings. I can't put my finger on my maternal grandfather's middle name, or how many minutes my grandmother's cinnamon rolls should stay in the oven, no matter how deliberately I try to clear a spot in my pre-frontal lobe. But since I became a knitter, certain memories of the farm keep resurfacing like the soybeans that work themselves up from the black dirt of our fields year after year.

Sheep were always regular tenants on our family's four hundred acres, and with their low bleats and gentle natures, I considered them wonderful company. They seemed to add a comforting sense of community to our relatively deserted part of the world and they even provided some quiet entertainment while I did my chores. Over a sink full of soapy water and dirty dishes, I could watch from the window the modest flock of seventy-five black-muzzled Suffolks grazing in the barnyard. While picking raspberries from the bushes in the west windbreak, I could see them playing follow-the-leader from pasture to pasture until they had worn down the high grass into a neat path. The sheep were simple and unassuming, and, unlike the pigs that our neighbors the Sullivans kept, they didn't smell so bad either. Although Billy Sullivan would breathe in deeply, turn around in his seat, and loudly declare to me, "Ahhh . . . the smell of money!" whenever our big, yellow school bus passed a pig farm, I thought I'd just as well be in the poorhouse and stick with sheep.

One Sunday after church, when I was about seven years old, my dad stuck his head in my bedroom doorway and mischievously said, "Why don't you get changed—I could use your help outside." I saw that he had traded his suit coat for coveralls, so I put on jeans and a well-worn sweater and hurried to fetch my own little coveralls that hung from a coat hook at the top of the basement stairs. I loved any chance I had to "help" my dear old dad with farm work and I ran to catch up with him. We climbed over a rickety fence and headed out to the sheep barn where his fellow Farm Bureau member, Mr. Johansen, was waiting for us with a set of shiny metal shears. It was sheep-shearing day!

To a seven year-old, the production of shearing sheep was full of drama. First, each animal had to be caught, which could prove to be a difficult task (as I knew from multiple times spent trying and failing to catch one to use as a makeshift pony). While the elderly Mr. Johansen and I looked on, Dad heroically trailed, tackled, and transferred each ewe to a pen in the barn. For me, witnessing his strategic weaving and maneuvering was like watching the world's greatest linebacker, and I cheered appropriately. Then, Dad held the sheep, one at a time, and talked soothingly in their ears while Mr. Johansen sheared off their oatmeal-colored coats of wool, exposing the white underneath. Each small pile of wool was thrown into a big, burlap sack that hung like a tube sock from a six-foot-high rack. After twenty-five or so sheep had given up their wool and the sack was almost full, I learned why I had been summoned to assist in the proceedings.

Dad and I climbed a ladder next to the tall sack, and then he picked me up and tossed me into the sack. I sunk down into the warmth of the wool and Dad laughed, "Go on, jump!"

It was better than a trampoline. I couldn't reach any great heights as I leapt up and down, compressing the wool to make room for more, but the experience was like a dream. I was enclosed in a giant, soft cocoon that could have come from the pages of *Alice in Wonderland*, and the air around me was filled with the sweet, heady scent of alfalfa. Unlike the cottony clouds my first-grade classmates and I drew to represent sheep's wool, the real stuff was dense and heavy, causing me to work up a sweat as I panted and marched high-kneed on top of it. Dad and Mr. Johansen threw in more and more wool, until I had packed it down as much as I could and had risen to the top of the burlap bag. This process was repeated again and again until every member of the flock was finally shorn.

When the work was done, Dad and Mr. Johansen stood outside the barn door in the low March sun and chatted about the weather or the price of corn. I stood with them, nodding and drinking Coke out of a sea-glass-colored bottle, proud to be part of this accomplished team. After Mr. Johansen pulled away in his dark blue pick-up, my father and I lingered to watch the sheep mill around the barnyard and bend their heads to reach the spring's first shoots of grass. Free from the grit of her matted winter wool, each ewe seemed to model her new white coat on lighter hooves. As Dad and I walked back to the house, we talked over the events of the afternoon, and I slipped my fingers into his callused hand, made soft by the wool's lanolin.

Years later—after high school, college, graduate school, and a few years in the working world—I found out my dad had been diagnosed with leukemia. The L word became a heavy weight that never left my chest. I imagine that it's always a shock for a daughter to realize the vulnerability of her father, especially one that could so deftly outrun a member of the wild (or at least not entirely tame) kingdom. When the bad news came, I had just completed my first knitting class and was working on the second in what would become a series of patterned, plain, striped, or textured hats. For several weeks, I ended each day by picking up my needles and knitting stitch after stitch after stitch. The wooden needles made rhythmic, muted clicks against each other; the charcoal wool under my fingers felt soft and dense, just the way it had the day I sheared sheep with my dad. Knitting became a comforting meditation that, in its own way, helped to lessen the weight of his diagnosis.

The following Christmas, I flew back to the farm and extended my stay so I could go with Dad to his first chemotherapy appointment—probably as much for my own peace of mind as for his. He, my mom, and I drove thirty minutes to the hospital, filling the space with surprisingly normal conversation and stories. In the room where he would receive treatment, the hospital had provided a kind of industrial easy chair, with silver IV racks alongside. Dad settled into the mechanized recliner and whistled approvingly.

"They even gave me a window seat," he announced.

"Best seat in the house," I replied.

Mom retired to the waiting room, and I busied myself by scanning the medical brochures on the table, monitoring the parking lot outside, and checking Dad's glass to see if he needed more water. Dad picked up the fat remote control and began to *click, click, click* through the one-hundred-and-one channels on the TV attached to the far wall. When it was time for chemo to begin, a brusque but likeable nurse shooed me to the waiting room, explaining that I could come back later. I found Mom next to a stack of *Ladies' Home Journal* and *Good Housekeeping* magazines and watched her *flip, flip, flip* through the pages. She looked up from her lap, paused for a moment, and said, "Maybe you need ice cream."

I realized at that moment that what I really could have used was my knitting bag. While Dad *click, click, clicked* and Mom *flip, flip, flipped*, I could have *knit, knit, knit*. All three of us were searching for something normal and controllable on which we could focus our attention during the strange hours ahead. Why hadn't I brought my knitting? Didn't I love the craft because it was something I could pick up and take anywhere? Hadn't my knitting accompa-

- - - -

nied me to the airport, the beach, the salon, and softball games? It would have fit right in at the clinic. Across the room, there was a comfortable-looking navy chair next to a floor lamp that would shed excellent light on a knitting project. I thought about what I would especially like to work on at that moment: something superlatively easy that didn't require too much brainpower—something in garter stitch on big, size 11 needles. Concentrating on steadily shifting stitches from left to right, I wouldn't necessarily notice the man—not much older than my dad—being wheeled down the hospital corridor as he put a mask to his face to help him breathe. With needles working in rhythm and precision, I wouldn't think too much about the girl of only nine or ten whose skin looked so pale against the colorful bandana wrapped around her head.

In the end, with my knitting bag tucked inside my suitcase back at the farm, I had to settle for ice cream; but for a knitter, even chocolate can't compete with the comfort of one hundred grams of yarn. As I sat across from Mom at a Culver's restaurant pushing my ice cream around its bowl until it began to melt, my fingers itched for thick needles and a woolen skein, soft and dense as the fleece from our old flock of sheep.

- - - -

Over the next several months, I knit a few baby hats and started a shawl, and Dad continued chemotherapy. One by one, my projects were completed, and little by little, his white-blood-cell counts improved. I know it was the medicine making him better, but to a Midwestern girl raised in the Methodist church, working those stitches was the closest thing I had to praying the rosary. Each knit and each purl was like another bead on which to meditate, my own words replacing the *Hail Marys* and *Our Fathers*. Mixed in with those prayerful thoughts were memories of all the things I've loved about my dad: how he snuck Reese's Peanut Butter Cups into my winter-coat pockets; how he woke me up in the middle of the night to witness meteor showers; and, of course, how he tossed me into a burlap sack with piles and piles of freshly shorn wool.

Maybe I'll knit my dear old dad something of his own for Christmas this year—a thick, warm scarf made from undyed oatmeal-colored wool perhaps—so he can wear it to remember me and the Sunday in March we spent shearing sheep. He has always claimed that there's nothing like the present, but I think some things are worth remembering. I only hope that after a summer of knitting inactivity, I haven't forgotten how to cast on. . . .

DUMPING GUILT

BY KAY DORN

Sometimes the solution to a problem you've been struggling with is so obvious it is easy to overlook. This is true for writer Kay Dorn, who discovers that her path to total relaxation is through knitting, not yoga. Kay's essays have appeared in *Knit Lit: Sweaters and Their Stories . . . and Other Writing about Knitting*, published by Three Rivers Press in 2002; *KnitLit (too): Stories from Sheep to Shawl . . . and More Writing about Knitting,* also by Three Rivers Press, in 2004; and *For the Love of Knitting: A Celebration of the Knitter's Art,* published by Voyageur Press in 2004.

D id your Mom tell you, as mine did, that the road to hell is paved with good intentions? If that is so, I was headed in the wrong direction: for years, I intended to start practicing yoga. Annually I called to learn class schedules. One year I didn't attend because we were having too much company. The next season I was taking a writing course and I didn't have time. Another year I was volunteering at the library and didn't want to take on anything extra.

Obviously, I was procrastinating, and it made me feel so guilty. I asked myself: why do I need yoga? I feel great. My regular morning stretching and weight exercises keep me flexible. I walk three miles every day, swim a half-mile in winter, and bike in the summer, so I don't need exercise. But I did have those tension headaches. And although yoga may have been just what I needed to relieve the tension—I just couldn't accept that the mind and body could be so intertwined that yoga could be the answer.

I told myself I wasn't the meditating type. My need to be always accomplishing something keeps my mind in upheaval. It's a compulsion: even when I'm doing something, my mind is deciding what I will start next. When I get in bed at night, before I can sleep I must review what I accomplished that day, then decide what I will do when I awake.

I need something to empty my mind occasionally, but I've never been able to just sit still and meditate—I've tried, and I'm a total wreck, thinking of what I *should* be doing. My daughter and more than one of my friends have suggested yoga would be the answer. In fact, they nagged me about it—hence my guilt for not trying it.

Then the Eureka! hit me.

– – – –

165

A while back I was having one of those days—waiting for a doctor's call, company coming, income tax to be finished—you know what I mean. My mind was whirling, my head pounding. Where to start? I couldn't concentrate on anything. I slumped into a comfy armchair—the one next to my knitting basket. But I *never* knit in the daytime, I thought, that's my night activity.

But for some reason that day I picked up the size 8 needles and spoke aloud to keep my mind focused, "Knit 1, purl 1, knit 1, purl 1," as I seed-stitched along the border of a baby blanket. Unlike my evening knitting, when the television is on or my husband is reading to me, the room was silent and I was alone. My mind turned to the joy of an expected grandchild, a prayer for his good health, and then back to when my children were babies. I wasn't practicing formal relaxation techniques, but I was definitely starting to relax.

My shallow breathing changed to deep, relaxed breaths. Tension seeped out. Time disappeared. As I began the basket-weave pattern of the blanket, my voice lowered to a whisper: "Knit 5, purl 5, knit 5, purl 5." I was quiet inside, and happy I had accomplished something. I had collapsed into the chair exhausted and emerged feeling calm and serene.

– – – –

Why had something so obvious eluded me? Why had I always saved this comfort until evenings when my world was bombarded with television and the telephone ringing and conversation? Why can't I knit in the seclusion of my quiet afternoons? I began to understand why even my guilt wasn't enough to push me to start yoga. "Knit, purl, knit purl" is the mantra of my hands. For me, knitting is as spiritual as it is physical. I have come to accept that even though dreams, anxieties, love, and anger can't be seen on an X-ray—there *is* a relationship between mind and body. I may be knitting a gift for someone (and fulfilling that need for accomplishment), but I am also doing something for myself.

Probably a "real" Yogi would scoff. But when I take up the yarn and needles in solitude, I tap into my spiritual side, and my mind is at peace. And in that sense, knitting *is* my yoga.

ANIMAL COMFORT

BY SUSAN GORDON LYDON

In this essay by author Susan Gordon Lydon, the calming effects of knitting extend beyond the creator. The luxurious, lace shawl she knits using qiviut yarn is also a great source of comfort for a friend. "Animal Comfort" was first printed earlier this year in Susan's book, *Knitting Heaven and Earth: Healing the Heart with Craft,* published by Broadway Books. Susan is also the author of *The Knitting Sutra, Craft as a Spiritual Practice,* published by Broadway Books in 2004, and *Take the Long Way Home: Memoirs of a Survivor,* published by HarperCollins in 1993.

For about ten years I've been going to the Russian River resort area in Northern California at the end of July with my friend Lou and her family. We stay at a place called Summerhome Park, situated at a bend in the green snakey river. Hills of redwood trees rise from its banks, and the air,

- - - -

carrying the combined fragrances of redwood, bay, and running river water, is so fresh and clean you wish you could bottle it and bring it home.

I sleep in the cabin with Lou's sister-in-law, Tina, and over the years a small group of what I've come to call cranky middle-aged women have emerged as a core of regular yearly guests. Besides Lou, who's been my closest friend for over a decade, and me, the group includes Tina and her longtime friend Theresa, who are both labor and delivery nurses.

Each year I watch the passage and progress of an osprey or a family of ospreys that appears precisely around the bend in the river each morning and late afternoon to fish. It announces its presence with a distinctive whistle my father taught me to recognize on one of our birdwatching trips to the Everglades, and is always an exhilarating sight. I once observed the parent ospreys taking their fledgling children on a trial flight, leading them on with a fish skeleton one parent held in its mouth.

Summerhome Park is one of those resorts built in the 1920s or 1930s, when wealthy families from San Francisco went to the Russian River to summer. It is an idyllic place for children, woodsy and mysterious, with a wide, safe beach, a lodge where teens can hang out buying candy and hamburgers and shooting pool, and many secluded spots along the river for canoeing, fishing, and Huck Finn–type imaginative wilderness adventures.

While the kids are hanging out at the lodge or around campfires on the beach, we women play a card game called Spite and Malice. It is a complicated form of multihanded solitaire. I'm sure Spite and Malice got its name from the viciously competitive way it must be played. The game's objective is to get rid of your pile of cards before anyone else, and one way of doing it is by purposely blocking your opponents' progress. Since Tina learned it from an elderly woman she helps care for named Lucille, we call the game Lucille.

In the long, lazy evenings after dinner, we women play many games of Lucille at the river. I am a bridge player and can endure almost anything with good games of cards. I used to say that the best thing about being in jail was that there were always enough people to play cards with, and in the course of many stays in rehab, I survived by playing spades, a simpler form of bridge, with my fellows. When I was a child on Long Island, and hurricanes or thunderstorms knocked out our power and flooded the only bridge to town, my father would light candles and play long games of canasta or Steal the Old Man's Bundle with the kids.

- - - -

Theresa came to Summerhome Park as a child. Her aunt and uncle owned a small general and grocery store she helped out in. It has long been boarded up, though still scenic, since we discovered Summerhome Park and began to go there.

I don't know that Tina, who is good-hearted and generous almost to a fault, would describe herself as cranky. But Theresa's eccentricities would make her embrace the description wholeheartedly. Together, the four of us generate a powerful female energy that reminds me of matriarchs in an elephant or buffalo herd. I once saw a buffalo cow give birth in Golden Gate Park. The other females surrounded her in a circle of protection. That is the sort of energy we possess.

Of course I bring my knitting to the river. One year I was experimenting with luxury materials. I had begun to knit with a fiber known as qiviut that had recently come onto the commercial market. Qiviut is spun from the downy underhair of the musk ox, a shaggy Arctic beast that roams the frozen tundra and puts one in mind of a smaller, stubbier version of the woolly mammoth.

The animal is little changed from the Ice Age. According to an article by Donna Druchunas in the Fall 2003 issue of *Interweave Knits*, the musk ox, which was hunted nearly to extinction in the 1860s, lives in remote areas of Greenland, Alaska, and Canada, "where it grows an under-wool that is . . . eight times warmer than sheep's wool. This layer of qiviut protects the animals in -100 degrees F weather; in fact, captive herds must be protected from over-heating when temperatures rise to just 70 degrees F."

To the Alaskan Yupiit people, the animal is known as "oomingmak" (the bearded one). And qiviut, the yarn spun from its soft, downy underfleece, is said to be finer, warmer, and lighter than cashmere. "With each animal producing just five to seven pounds of qiviut each year," Druchunas wrote, "the fiber remains rare and expensive." There are cooperatives of Inuit women in the Yukon who make gar-ments from qiviut and sell them by mail order. They are costly and exquisite. But the fiber only became available for the home knitter in the past decade when a woman named Nancy Bender began raising musk oxen on a farm in Hamilton, Montana, and having the underfleece spun into yarn.

At about the same time, a company somewhere began producing luxurious knitting needles made of rosewood and ebony. I bought a pair of ebony straight needles with rose-wood knobs and imagined myself knitting qiviut on ebony in the very height of luxury.

– – – –

The needles didn't work out too well for me. The wood was hard and hurt my hands. But the qiviut worked out fine.

It was at that time only available in a taupey brown color, the natural color of the fleece, a color that seemed as though it would be comforting in a cozy animal way. Warmth-for-weight ratio is a big deal in the fiber world. Mohair for instance has a very high degree of warmth for its light weight, and cashmere has been coveted for years because of this quality. Of course not all cashmere is created equal. The diet of the goats, the altitude at which they are raised, the processing of the fleece, and the spinning, as well as the raw fleece itself, make the feel of the fiber vary widely.

Downy fibers such as qiviut and cashmere possess what is called a "halo," the fine hairs that surround the core of spun fiber and make it more or less fuzzy depending on the yarn. They are also said to "bloom" with washing. As the fiber absorbs water and the tightness of the spin relaxes, the yarn fluffs up and softens in an appealing way. This works particularly well with lace patterns, as the halo blooms and occupies the empty spaces formed by the yarnovers or holes in the lace.

By this point, I had been knitting so much and so

passionately that I had caught up with most new developments in the knitting world, had become current, as it were, and was hungry for novelty and variety.

I had found a pattern in a book of classic British Isles knitwear for a lace shawl that was pictured wrapped around a baby. It didn't look very large. I ordered a couple of skeins of qiviut from Nancy Bender and began knitting my first lacy shawl. Did I mention that the yarn was extravagantly pricey? It made cashmere look like a bargain.

The shawl was in the pattern known as feather and fan, or old shale, which makes a scallopy edge to the design. Though it was not the first time I knitted lace, it was the first of many shawls I was to knit and started me on a major binge of lace shawl knitting. This piece had a simple triangular shape rather than the large squares I would later make, and featured only one lace pattern rather than the varying patterns of the others.

Who knows why one pattern feels so pleasurable and comfortable to knit while another feels frustrating and irritating? This for me is one of the enduring mysteries of lace knitting. But the rhythm and feel of the feather and fan appealed to me right from the start. I loved the rhythm of its yarnovers and decreases, the mathematical arabesque of adding and subtracting stitches, the alternating columns and arches that appeared with each repetition of the pattern.

But the quantity of yarn required for the piece had not been precisely delineated in the instructions, and its finished size had been concealed in the folds wrapped around the baby. So I kept running out of yarn. Every week it seemed I was calling Nancy Bender to tell her I needed more qiviut while the price for the project mounted ever upward. Also, since the fleece had been gathered from different animals and was only available in its natural color, the skeins did not match exactly in color, weight, or the finish of the thread.

Some were lighter in color, some darker, some smoother, some fluffier, with a shaggier feel more like mohair.

I was about midway through the shawl when I went to the Russian River that year, in 1997, and the price of the yarn had already soared to about $250.00, with no end in sight.

Theresa pulled it right out of my knitting bag. "What is this?" she demanded as the shawl fluffed up into its shaggy, lacey, animal beauty. "I want this," she said. "I have to have it."

"I can't possibly sell it for what the materials cost," I said. "The yarn has already cost $250 and I'm nowhere near finished."

"I would pay you five or six hundred dollars for something like this," she said. Theresa lives near the ocean in San Diego. Both her husband and her daughter are avid surfers. She was already imagining the comforting fluffy shawl wrapped around her shoulders on chilly evenings at the beach.

When it was finished, I sold it to her. To my exacting knitter's eye, the shawl was far from perfect. There were mistakes in the lace, so the columns and arches didn't line up precisely. The color wasn't uniform, as it would be if one were to buy all the yarn at one time, in the same dye lot. It varied from light to dark, from finer to thicker, from smooth to furry in various parts.

The shape was asymmetrical, and the size somewhere between a shawl and a scarf, not the generous enveloping wrap I'm sure Theresa had imagined. I hadn't yet learned how to block lace, so it was lumpy and bumpy. It possessed plenty of that quality the Japanese call *wabi sabi*, the charm of the imperfect.

But Theresa didn't think so.

"I don't know what I ever did to deserve anything as beautiful as this," she said. "But it must have been good."

In truth the shawl was cozy and comforting, not so very far from the animals that had given their downy underhair to create the yarn, and of course it had absorbed all that female energy that the four of us, plus Tina's other nurse friends, generated on the river.

It was also the first time I had ever been paid what I thought was a fair price for my labor and materials.

Theresa loved it. She kept it in a special box. Enshrined, as she said, like the relic of a saint. And since she, Tina, and Lou all grew up in Roman Catholic families, Theresa thought of a singularly Catholic use for the shawl.

"This is the sort of thing," she said, "that I want to be wearing in my open casket."

"I never would have thought of that," I said, "but now that you mention it, it seems fine."

Over the years we've been going to the Russian River all of us have lost members of our families. Lou lost a brother; Tina lost both parents and two brothers; Theresa's brother and my father all have died. Though we are only together for a short, intense time each year, we have used our connection and companionship to mourn and console, to comfort and succor one another. We have shared the deaths in our families that have occurred between each season.

Theresa, who is from a large Mexican family, liked to regale us with stories about her late brother Louie, who had been something of an outlaw and reprobate. He rode a Harley, trafficked in illicit substances, and had a large number of girlfriends who streamed through the house in a steady procession as he lay dying upstairs of liver disease.

"Louie's fools," Theresa called them. According to Theresa, the women remained devoted to Louie even though she did everything in her power to dissuade them. "You don't want to go up there," she would tell one of them, "Mary Jo is already there and you know how much you hate her."

"I couldn't really blame them," Theresa said, "because Louie was so appealing. But I'm glad I was his sister, so I didn't have to be one of his fools."

The women mourned en masse at Louie's funeral, a colorful affair which naturally featured the deceased in an open casket. Some of Louie's buddies had thoughtfully provided him with some sustenance for the afterlife, several joints of marijuana placed in the breast pocket of his shirt.

Seeing this, Theresa marched right up to the casket and took the joints out of Louie's pocket, "because," as she said, "he wouldn't be needing them where he was going, and I needed them right then."

Theresa and Tina saw each other between times at the river, and Lou and I lived close to each other at home, but the four of us rarely gathered except at the river. One winter Lou went with Tina to San Diego, and Theresa conducted what she called "a showing" of the shawl in its special box.

Tina's mother had been ill and on dialysis for some time, but when she died suddenly, Tina was devastated. Theresa wasn't able to attend the funeral. But she offered Tina what, to her mind, was the next best consolation to her presence.

"I told her I was sorry I couldn't come to the funeral," she said. "But I said she could borrow the shawl to wear."

She called it "the shawl," as though it were the only one in the world and everyone would know what she meant. As though it possessed magical powers. As though it could function as an intermediary between worlds, between animals and humans, between the living and the dead.

For Tina and Theresa, who were so often present at the mysteries of birth, the occasions of birth and death required a kind of animal comfort. The swaddling of the baby. The shrouding of the corpse. The wearing of a magic shawl to ease the pain of grief. All these times demanded a kind of bundling or wrapping that would somehow aid the body's passage between the states of being and nonbeing.

A shawl is a garment to be wrapped around the wearer. It envelopes the person in warmth. It is a natural garment for the contemplative nature of knitting. Prayer Shawl Ministries have now sprung up in many areas of the country. They are groups who knit for a member in distress, stitching their work with prayer and positive intention. Then they wrap the recipient in the shawl as a blessing.

The last time I saw Theresa, she told me she had loaned the qiviut shawl to her mother. Her mother suffers from lymphoma, and Theresa thought the shawl might ease the pain of the tumors in her neck.

Theresa's mother is something of a fancy lady. According to Theresa, she never goes out even to do her gardening in anything but nylon hose and immaculate Ferragamos. Now she has a shaggy, imperfect, hand-stitched shawl to warm the achings of her heart and her neck. And since the shawl has a life of its own, like a child you've given birth to, she will probably never know it comes to her courtesy of the great, shambling Arctic beasts whose coats provided the yarn, and the nimble fingers of the knitter that was me.

- - - -

A KNITTER'S THERAPY

BY SUZYN JACKSON

In her essay "A Knitter's Therapy," writer and expert multitasker Suzyn Jackson finds that knitting is the perfect antidote for her racing mind. Suzyn lives in Maryland, where she writes, knits, and designs jewelry. Her passions include fine art, Dumas, the southeast corner of Central Park, and red socks. Her essay "Knit-Surfing the Subway" appeared in *For the Love of Knitting: A Celebration of the Knitter's Art,* published by Voyageur Press in 2004.

I'm the kind of person whose brain runs on several channels at a time. I often burn dinner. I start with the best of intentions, but by the time the pan has heated, I've had five different thoughts and acted on three of them. I've tried to meditate. I have tried to release these thoughts into the great unknown, to seek peace in tranquility. I can't do it. But I can knit.

People knit for many reasons—creative expression, gifts of love, to prove that they can. I knit for all of these reasons and more: Knitting is my therapy. Knitting is my meditation.

- - - -

The quiet geometry of stitches, the dance of color, and the soft yielding yarn displace the thoughts that I cannot release.

My senior year of college, I had a full course load, an honors thesis, a part-time job, a role in a play, and a stinky boyfriend. I didn't realize he was stinky. Everyone else did, but I, young and naive, had promised to love him forever and I thought that I meant it. Until one day, when I still thought that I would love him forever, but I also knew that I never wanted to speak to him again, and I told him so.

Now, you might have thought that the courses and the thesis and the job and the play would have been enough to keep me occupied, but no—I still had a brain channel free, and it was all stinky boyfriend, all the time. I cried a lot. I had a habit of blasting classical music while I studied, but not even Glenn Gould could drown out the keening chatter: Had I done the right thing? What about the promises (young, naive promises!) that I'd made? Should I just pick up the phone?

Instead, I picked up my knitting needles. I discovered that if I stuck to plain stockinet, I could knit pretty much by touch. This meant that I could read, knit, and play loud Bach at the same time. It worked! It was enough to keep my brain occupied. For the next month, if I wasn't typing, walking, eating, or on stage, I was knitting. Smooth cotton, simple geometry, and the hidden wisdom of my fingers kept me sane. By the end of the month, I had knit two-and-a-half cute, boxy

- - - -

t-shirts. More importantly, I had lived without stinky for a month. It was clear to me then that if I could live without him for a month, I could live without him for a year, a decade, a lifetime.

Over the next several years, I lived in many cities and took many jobs. I went through times when I knitted constantly, and times when I hardly knitted at all. But I always had a full stash of yarn and several projects going, even if they'd lain untouched for months. Eventually I landed in New York, where I met and married the man of my dreams. We lived in a little Manhattan apartment and thought we were pretty swish. Then I got pregnant. With a little one on the way, we decided to be sensible and move closer to family, somewhere not quite so expensive.

On moving day, six months pregnant and forbidden from lifting anything, I dashed across the street to pick up sandwiches and coffee. (Perhaps "dashed" is the wrong word, but I could still achieve a New York–paced waddle.) I found myself at the Sav-a-thon, one of those New York stores that sell plastic tablecloths and vacuums and gilded crystal roses and itchy acrylic by the pound. In a corner, I found some fluffy pink and purple yarn and I bought it.

Three days later, I sat in my country-kitchen-cum-ballroom, in the eerie suburban quiet, listening to the coffee drip. How many gallons of coffee had I made in New York and never heard it drip? I was completely lost. All the New York skills I'd so carefully honed were useless. You can't dip and weave your way through rush hour (without spilling your deli coffee) in a place where there are no delis, no subways, no crowds. The grocery store was half a mile away and the nearest anything else was even farther, and I wasn't sure I could remember how to drive. I was no longer operating on several channels—my pregnant brain had one, and it was on overload. The baby kicked and a tidal wave of hormones threatened to obliterate my savvy self, leaving behind a snuffling sobbing lump . . .

But I knew where I'd tucked the pink and purple fluff. And, miraculously, I knew where my knitting needles were in the mountain of cardboard boxes. I didn't need Bach and a book this time. I sat in my enormous, silent kitchen and made a scarf for my niece. The stripes, for some reason, started going on an angle, but that was okay. It wasn't the most accomplished thing I'd made, by a long shot, but it was pretty. In that gleaming, echoing house it was something familiar, something that was mine, an anchor to all my former selves. Somehow that little pink and purple scarf made all the other changes bearable.

Others might swear by psychoanalysis, yoga, or antidepressant drugs. As I weather life's storms, I will keep my knitting needles close by.

– – – –

LISTEN TO YOUR KNITTING

BY MEG SWANSEN

For master knitter and writer Meg Swansen, knitting is a way of life. With knitting needles in hand, she not only finds peace and tranquility, she makes unanticipated and exciting discoveries that enrich her knitwear designs.

Meg is the owner of Schoolhouse Press, a publisher of knitting books and videos and a source for knitting notions, wool, pattern kits, and books. She is the author of several books about knitting, including *Sweaters from Camp, Meg Swansen's Knitting, Handknitting with Meg Swansen,* and *A Gathering of Lace.* She also writes a regular column for *Vogue Knitting* and heads up four weeks of knitting camp each summer.

Today is a rather typical one at Schoolhouse Press: in the office the phone is ringing, a fax is coming in, and Eleanor is packing up knitting books, wool, and videos to be mailed out to domestic and worldwide destinations. I am in an adjacent room, sitting in my Knitting Chair by the woodstove with a cup of tea (it is winter and we are in Wisconsin). A cat is curled up next to me, the sun is streaming in over my shoulder, and my feet are comfortably up on the coffee table as I knit . . . I am at work. Why is there not an English term that defines "work" as being able to earn one's living while engaged in a fulfilling, imaginative, and satisfying occupation that realizes one's heart's desire? Well, that may be a bit strong, but you know what I mean.

Knitting practically fills my entire life. I spend most of my waking moments either knitting or thinking about it. Having been involved with this topic so deeply for so many decades, I have gathered scores of stories from other knitters about the power and salvation this craft has brought to their lives; how they have been able to survive troubled times only because of the soothing, comforting, and meditative aspects of the knitting in their hands. There are even several books devoted to the philosophical nature of hand knitting.

- - - -

I have always espoused and supported this important part of knitting, but during the time of greatest grief in my own life, I was unable to knit a stitch for several months. This surprised me very much, as it ran counter to my belief. However, it happened only once, and I still make sure I have knitting in my hands for run-of-the-mill occasions of sadness, stress, or general upset, as well as for all the joyful and contented times of my life, which, I hasten to add, are the more plentiful.

What is it about knitting that makes it so appealing? Is it the repetitive and hypnotic movement of your hands? Is it the ability to put your hands on autopilot and mentally escape the reality of the moment? Is it the inner satisfaction of creativity? To attempt a description is almost futile, but each obsessive knitter knows (or rather, feels) the answer for themselves and, naturally, the answer varies from knitter to knitter.

Yes, knitting can be exceedingly comforting and calming—but it can also be exciting and riveting. To my mind, one main reason to knit is the endless possibilities this discipline offers. With wool and needles in your hands, you alone are in charge of what you will produce with them. These days there is a staggering array of materials to excite your imagination and, literally, hundreds of handknitting books to inspire you—traditional books on Norwegian color-pattern or Swedish two-end texture; Bavarian twisted stitch; British Fair Isle, Arans, Guernseys, and Shetland lace—plus scores of contemporary designs for knitted scarves, bags, hats, stockings, and sweaters. Debbie New's *Unexpected Knitting* stands alone as an example of untethered and joyful knitting—and she includes structured as well as totally freeform designs.

The excitement of knitting a new pattern can become all-consuming: when I came up with the charts for my first attempt at picture knitting (the Weeping Sun & Moon sweater), I was so thrilled to see what was emerging from my needles that I stayed up late and got up early; and, impatient to see what would happen next, I startled myself by finishing that garment in little more than a week.

Although I have tried, I do not have the ability to sketch a design, knit a swatch, note all the technical details, and send it to another knitter to be realized. This inability forces me to handknit each design myself, which is why my output is relatively slow. I cast on with a rough plan of the proposed journey, and I make discoveries along the way. Knitting myself into a corner may become the source of an "innovation" as I play the game of only ripping when absolutely necessary. The challenge of finding my way out of a predicament may take my knitting brain along a new path. Any number of times I have proven one of my favorite sayings: a repeated mistake may become a new design.

Occasionally knitting takes on a life of its own, so pay attention and listen to your knitting. The shape of the armholes or neckline may be determined by the texture or color-pattern motif on the body, and is not even subject to your input. For instance, when I create a mirror image of color pattern down the top of a sleeve, I do not bother to chart the design in advance—I simply center the motif at the shoulder seam line, establish the double-decrease frequency, then watch, mesmerized, as new heretofore-undreamed-of Rorschach-like designs begin to appear. The same bit of magic occurs when you face the necessity of mirror-imaging a very large motif at the side "seams" of a sweater body on a circular needle: as long as the main pattern is perfectly centered fore and aft, it matters not where you have to break the motif when you reach the seam. Simply use that stitch as a pivot point, work the same chart line back in the opposite direction, and marvel at the wonderful new design that appears along the sides. You can hardly go wrong, so relax, be consistent, and the pattern will take care of itself. I often tell people that they are in charge of their knitting, but considering the above, I see that, frequently, knitting is in charge of itself.

As you accumulate more and more techniques, you are able—in almost direct proportion—to achieve the ability to knit whatever you like. For me, exciting and riveting doesn't even begin to describe it.

Chapter 6

GETTING HOOKED ON CROCHET, KNITTING'S SECOND-COUSIN

"CROCHET BECAME AN OBSESSION. . . . MY INITIAL FAS-
CINATION WAS WITH USING A HOOK TO CREATE A FAB-
RIC BY USING JUST ONE LIVE LOOP AT A TIME: INSERTING
A HOOK THROUGH LOOPS ALREADY MADE, PULLING UP
NEW LOOPS, SECURING THOSE NEW LOOPS WITH STILL
ADDITIONAL LOOPS, AND THEN STARTING THE SEQUENCE
ALL OVER AGAIN WHEN I HAD JUST ONE LOOP LEFT ON
MY HOOK. THERE WAS A RHYTHM TO THE MECHANICS.
EACH SINGLE STITCH, EACH PATTERN GROUP OF STITCHES,
EACH PROJECT HAD ITS OWN RHYTHM."

—*Jennifer Hansen, "The Rhythm and the Destiny of Living Loops," 2005*

Crochet stories in a book of knitting essays? Everyone knows that real knitters look down their noses at crochet and would never touch a crochet hook unless they needed to pick up a few dropped stitches, right? Think again. These days, it's just as common to see people crocheting at the local coffee shop as it is to catch a glimpse of a knitter happily stitching away. More and more knitters have been picking up crochet hooks to learn how to add pretty finishing touches to afghans, sweaters, and hats, while those who learned to crochet long ago are revisiting the craft. And, just as many who are new to *both* needle arts choose to learn crochet as those who opt for knitting needles. So it makes perfect sense to include a chapter on crochet in this book. After all, knitting and crochet are simply different means to the same end: a beautiful, handmade garment.

THE RHYTHM AND THE DESTINY OF LIVING LOOPS

BY JENNIFER HANSEN

Writer Jennifer Hansen sees no reason why anyone should have to choose between crochet and knitting. Instead, she urges crafters to look at each project individually and ask the question, would this [sweater, poncho, scarf, etc.] look better as a crocheted or a knitted garment?

Jennifer is the founder and chief creative force behind Stitch Diva Studios (www.stitchdiva.com), a company that specializes in fashion-forward knit and crochet patterns. Her fresh perspective on knitting and crochet has been featured in various online publications as well as in the magazines *Vogue Knitting* and *Crochet!* and the book *Contemporary Crochet,* published by Lark Books in 2005.

M y first love was crochet. Before becoming pregnant,
I was never attracted to, never noticed, and certainly never considered trying a needle art. In fact I'd considered crochet a quaint anachronistic throwback for
people—mostly women—who had nothing better to do
with their time.

But my pregnancy was prompting me to not only re-
evaluate my perceptions of "domestic," but some of my fundamental life choices and interests as well. Most importantly, my hormone-induced restlessness and insomnia
needed diversion. I became receptive.

It was my friend Jan who taught me to crochet. When
she told me she crocheted, I remember thinking it must be
like macramé. I had no recognition of the craft, and certainly considered it to be very different from the architec-
ture and technology that comprised my background. In a
several-hour session at her home, Jan taught me the basics.
I went to the craft store, bought some yarn, and within a
week I had crocheted a massive, uneven, and very ugly blanket. By the time that blanket was done, I had discovered
the rhythm, mindset, and muscle memory of crochet. To
my absolute amazement, I had become a crocheter.

Crochet became an obsession. I worked through the
wonder and anticipation of a first pregnancy by crocheting

- - - -

an entire hope chest of clothing for my son. My initial fascination was with using a hook to create a fabric by using just one live loop at a time: inserting a hook through loops already made, pulling up new loops, securing those new loops with still additional loops, and then starting the sequence all over again when I had just one loop left on my hook. There was a rhythm to the mechanics. Each single stitch, each pattern group of stitches, each project had its own rhythm. As I was able to master a project and learned to immerse myself in the rhythm of the mechanics to make it, I discovered that beyond just the rhythm, there was a rich connection about it too.

I felt an ageless link to the past, the present, and the future. A whole line of minds—engineering minds and artist minds and worrying minds—minds using their hands to establish a meditative rhythm that allowed them to drift away to a different place, and in the process creating a beautiful thing. For me, the meditation of every loop served to stave off the impatience of meeting the baby boy inside me, and helped me to transform my fear of childbirth into something tangible—a cloth made with my intent and my love to welcome my baby boy into the world. I imagined generations of women lying awake by candlelight, driven to create heirloom layettes for the same ageless reasons. It was

- - - -

art, it was utilitarian, it was engineering, it was construction, and I could do it anywhere. There was nothing quaint about it.

I began to realize that crochet was just one of several ways that you could loop a fabric together while transporting your mind to another place. So I went to the craft store and bought a learn-to-knit kit.

I made several ugly little projects that were full of dropped-stitch holes and uneven tension. It was so much easier to make a mistake in knit, and so much harder to correct it! Instead of just one loop, I was juggling scores. Instead of one hook, I had two needles to manipulate. This brutal craft undermined the muscle memory I had worked so hard to acquire in crochet—I couldn't find a rhythm when I couldn't even hold the needles without having my stitches fall off!

Comparing knitting to crochet was like comparing lovers; I was impatient and I judged knitting only by its difference to my first love, crochet. It was a poncho project that finally provided the breakthrough, a substantial enough project to provide a vast uninterrupted landscape of many hours of stitches. The long hours spent knitting wore me down; my critical mind with its comparisons was cleared. I felt the familiar meditation of the loops. My needles be-

– – – –

came sticks, spear-heading a dynamic fabric, and I was creating a surface of tiny interlocking chains. I could see the logic in the chains. The fabric that emerged from my needles was no longer marred by dropped stitches, and my tension was regulated with the harmony in my mind. I had discovered the rhythm of knit in the same way I had discovered the rhythm of crochet.

Now, when I meet a knitter who says they've tried crochet but just can't get the hang of it because it is feels so unnatural, or a crocheter who complains about knitting for the same reasons, I ask them how they felt about their craft when they started. Did mastery come overnight? Did mastery come while they compared what they were attempting to something else? Knitting and crochet each have their unique characteristics possibilities, and limitations. Sometimes one is preferable to the other to best achieve a certain result, and sometimes it is advantageous to combine the two to get the inherent strengths of both. Sure, you can finish your knitting with a little crochet flower or edging, and you may find that it's best to finish your crochet with a knit ribbing too. These are obvious strengths. But there are other possibilities for both crafts that are unobtainable if you don't let yourself become receptive to the other craft without preconception. In that possibility lies the future.

– – – –

In my reading on the history of knit and crochet, what strikes me is that what we term crochet and knitting in present day are but instances of continuously evolving crafts. Passed from practitioner to practitioner, the crafts have evolved, mutated, and advanced through world cultures, with countless variations. Whereas the origins of knitting seem to spring from before the first millennium, crochet seems to have evolved some time in the nineteenth century as a byproduct of tambour embroidery. I imagine today's knitting and crochet as sister permutations of a fundamental creative force to make looped fabric with simple, portable tools. That force allows the mind of the knitter or crocheter to roam free, surrounding them with a steady, self-made rhythm of creation.

The evolution of these crafts continues. In time, they may meld, diverge, or develop new hybrids in order to create exciting new fabrics and practices, with loops every bit as intentional as those we knit or crochet today. We are all here playing our part, with our hooks, our needles, our books, our stitch groups, and our websites. We are writing our chapter in the story of knitting and crochet, and in doing so we are perpetuating the gift of their eternal and ageless rhythms.

THE ROAD TO BECOMING THE FASTEST CROCHETER IN THE WORLD

BY LILY M. CHIN

Lily Chin confesses to being a really big ham. She has been the "poster child" for yarn crafts for the past decade, specializing in sound bites and putting forth a good "face" for knitters and crocheters at large. She has appeared in dozens of newspapers and on scores of television shows, including the *Late Show with David Letterman*. By participating in knitting and crocheting contests like the one described in this essay, she hopes to promote knitting and crochet. She is the author of *Knit and Crochet with Beads,* published by Interweave Press; *The Urban Knitter,* published by Berkley Books; and *Mosaic Magic* and *Afghans Made Easy,* both published by Oxmoor House.

First of all, I am probably *not* the fastest crocheter in the world. Sure, it's true that I'll soon be listed in the *Guinness Book of World Records* as the fastest crocheter to make it to the official competitions. But I'm sure there's someone out there, yet to be discovered, who crochets faster than me and who can whoop my butt!

That said, I am pretty speedy. So, how did I get that way? What are some of the secrets to my success?

A LITTLE MOTIVATION

I wouldn't have gotten where I am today without the help of my sister Amy. She and I are only a year apart. As kids, maybe when we were eight- and nine-years-old, we both learned to crochet. We'd then go on to race each other. Ah, nothing like sibling rivalry to light that fire underneath you. Thanks, Amy.

P.S. She no longer crochets!

JUST LIKE A COWGIRL NEEDS A SIX-SHOOTER WITH A STEADY AIM . . .

We crocheters have to look at our tools. I swear by and only use the Susan Bates aluminums with the "in-line" heads. I call them flat heads. Pulling through stitches is much easier and smoother with these hooks. Mind you, this may not be the case for everyone. Try out a few types of hooks to see which works best for you.

COUNT TEN PACES, TURN, AND TAKE AIM

We then have method. I hold the hook overhand style, much in the same way I hold a knife. Indelicate, perhaps, and certainly unladylike according to the Victorians, but this technique gives me better control and prevents the stress and strain that can lead to the dreaded CTS or RMS (that's carpel tunnel syndrome, and repetitive motion syndrome).

I hold the yarn in my left hand, looped over my left index finger. I hold my index finger up in the air as my left thumb and middle finger hold down my work in progress, providing tension. When I pick up a loop, my hook is faced up, but I flip my wrist and point my hook downward to draw any loops through. Thus, there is a lot of movement on the right wrist.

No matter what, I do not tension the yarn over the left pinkie first. I find that the looser I am, the faster I am. I'm a fast and loose woman, what can I say? Hee hee hee. Lack of tension speeds me up, more tension slows me down. I've been known to crochet worsted-weight yarn with a size G hook and still get a very loose gauge.

– – – –

With a Few Tricks Up Her Sleeve . . .

Now, here are the really sneaky tricks. I grease up my hooks—honest! I find that if I rub moisturizer or hand cream around the tip of my hook and then wipe it off with a tissue, the hook stays very slick, keeping the yarn moving along. (Actually, I've recently found that liquid soap is even more unctuous, and have resorted to using it instead!)

Don't forget how important music can be. It relieves a little pressure and can psyche out the opponent, which never hurts. Most importantly, music helps keep my rhythm going—the faster the song, the better. My personal preference is for the song "I Wanna Be Sedated" by the early '80s punk-rock band, the Ramones.

I usually do a few other things to try to psyche out opponents. I'll crochet a few stitches with my eyes closed, crack a few jokes, etc. Confidence and cocky self-assuredness can work wonders.

Lastly, I try to stay relaxed and to have fun when competing. I see the competition as enjoyment rather than a pressure situation. I just can't take it too seriously, lest the anxieties eat away at me.

SHOWDOWN AT THE OKAY CORRAL

Finally it is time to put all these skills and tricks to good use. All the national time-trials trained me well for the international match. My first "showdown" came in early October 2002 at New York City's "Knit Out and Crochet Too" event at Union Square Park. Wendy Moorby, the speediest English knitter, and Susan Briscoe, the fastest British crocheter, both came from the United Kingdom to face-off against me and Grace Judson, the quickest knitter in the United States.

I dressed the part, donning a felted cowboy hat (made especially for me by my good friend Bev Galeskas, of Fiber Trends patterns), cowboy boots, a crocheted western shirt, and holsters, which held my collection of crochet hooks! I brought along the music from the movie *The Good, The Bad, and the Ugly* for that fast-draw-at-high-noon-at-the-Okay-Corral mood and as an intimidation tactic, again, to psyche out the opponent.

It appeared to work, as Susan made a comment about how I seemed to have come with my own musical accompaniment . . . snicker. Once the stitching was underway, I played the music card again, requesting a fast track by my beloved Ramones, for keeping up the tempo. Lastly, upon winning with a score of 92.5 double-crochet stitches in the allotted three-minute's time (versus Susan's 76), I arranged for the deejay to play "We Are the Champions" by Queen.

ROUND TWO

Two years later, I went to London in early October for a rematch. The competition was to be held at the "Knitting and Stitching Show" in Alexandra Palace (or Ally Pally, as the locals refer to it), and the cast of characters had not changed much since the first showdown. Kaete Brady replaced Grace Judson as the fastest American knitter. Kaete was from New Hampshire, and I couldn't help but think of the irony that here I was from New York—Kaete and I were the new-world versions of original places in the United Kingdom.

I could not resist a little showboating at the pre-competition press conference. I crocheted blindfolded, behind my back, and between my legs! I should also mention that I wore my cowgirl outfit yet again, and I splurged on a new pair of cowboy boots for the competition. The United Kingdom may never be the same!

I think competition organizers were trying to psyche me out by having all kinds of last-minute changes. Once I got there, forgetting that they changed the *day* on me from Saturday to Friday, they then changed the *time* on me as well, from noon to 3:30. They claimed they were hoping for more entries for the challenge (i.e., they were hoping someone would come along who could do better than their existing champ and offer me a *real* challenge). Then they said no music allowed. This struck me funniest. Guess they would try *any*thing for some advantage.

As if this wasn't enough, they changed the yarn and hook size from double-knitting weight and G to Aran-weight and H. Before I left the states, I had actually practiced with the prescribed yarn and hook and came close to my own personal best of 98 dc in three minutes. I got 97.5 dc and was pretty confident, especially when I would be facing-off against the same woman as last time.

At the last minute, Susan Briscoe, the U.K. champ, suggested using this delicious merino-wool-, cashmere-, and angora-blend yarn, and I was willing. Yummy as it felt, however, we made a big mistake in working with it, as it was waaay too soft and squishy, and neither of us could control it well. To make matters worse, it was too HOT and sticky in the room and we were both wearing sweaters. Thus, Susan and I were both well under our records. I won with only 86 dc (remember, I did it with 92.5 last time) and Susan did a measly 63. My margin of victory increased, however, as the last time I had won by 16.5 dc, and this time the difference was 23 dc.

It was not my best performance, but at least my hubby was there to root for me and to take pictures. I had other friends there as well—Takako of Habu yarns, and other exhibitors at the show from the United States. I actually got a bigger round of applause because of the surprising number of U.S. ex-patriots (or ex-pats as they are called there) at the show. They were sooo sweet to come out and support us.

Epilogue

A week after successfully defending my title, I taught at the Creative Sewing and Needlecraft Festival in Toronto, where they held contests to find the fastest knitter and the fastest crocheter in Canada. One need not be Canadian to participate.

I finally broke the barrier and set not only a personal best, but a new world record.

My record used to be 98 double-crochet stitches in three minutes. For the past three years, my goal had been to break 100, and I finally did it. My new official score is 101 double-crochets in three minutes. It must have been the Canadian water (grin).

– – – –

POTHOLDER PRODIGY
MAKES GOOD

BY SIGRID ARNOTT

Writer Sigrid Arnott learned to crochet as a child and proceeded to churn out miles of single crochet chain—enough to get the craft out of her system . . . or so she thought. Sigrid is a knitter and crocheter who lives in Minneapolis, Minnesota.

Just because I grew up living a quarter mile up the road from my grandmother, don't think that I learned to crochet at her knee. It's true I did learn *because* of her, but definitely not *from* her.

My grandmother wasn't one of your typical grandma types who liked to sit around doing things with needles, hooks, and yarn. She *looked* like a proper grandma with her high-heeled oxfords, print dresses, and white hair in a grandmotherly bun, but she had qualities that made her rather . . . unusual. Even though she had lost some fingers on her left hand in a gun accident, she liked to sit on her porch with her rifle, not her needlework. "Gauge" referred to her preferred shotgun-shell size, not the number of stitches she made over four inches.

Luckily, I grew up on a ranch in a remote valley of central Montana, so not many people knew that my grandmother did her sewing positioned in front of a window, not to let in natural light but to provide armed surveillance over her garden. Should any innocent bunny rabbits dare nibble the lettuce growing in her extensive plots, she reached for the rifle kept next to the sewing machine, and shot them. She didn't *shoot at* them, she *shot* them—often smack dab between the eyes. Then she ate them.

Respect was not what I felt for her; it was more like sheer terror. When I asked her how old she was, she convinced me she was two hundred, and I believed this longer than I believed in the Easter Bunny. When I spent the night at her house, she woke me up in the morning with a unique method: before putting in her false teeth, she pulled her long white hair down over her face, crept right up to my bed, lowered her face six inches over mine, then yelled, "Boo!" In truth, I was less frightened by this technique than by what I imagined might possibly be her motivation.

- - - -

In turn, I always knew I was a disappointment to her. I didn't stand out in any positive way from my two older brothers, or from my three older cousins who lived another mile up the road. My schedule for passing childhood cognitive milestones was relaxed and unhurried: even with the help of my mother's flashcards, I only learned to talk at the age my older brother learned to *read*; a kindergarten I.Q. test indicated that I might be "trainable." Because I was afraid of my grandmother, I was even more tongue-tied than usual around her. My mother once heard her mutter about me, "Well, at least she's beautiful." It was as if my only hope was for some future man to be fooled by good looks into marrying someone mentally deficient.

Around the age of five, I suddenly developed a quality that made me stand out from the others: I became accident prone.

Although my parents seemed to think of me as just active—and unlucky—my grandmother saw a more alarming transformation from a slow-witted-but-cute girl into a petite female Scarface. A face-first fall from a pick-up truck into a dry riverbed fractured my skull and required a jagged line of stitches up my brow line. Another tumble killed my front tooth, turning it black. In a kindergarten carpool, I ran into a car door and needed to have my upper lip sewn up. An accidental head-on collision with a calf opened up a hole on my chin that was sutured. I remember the intent faces of doctors leaning over me as they carefully sewed me up and then, a few weeks later, plucked the black threads out of the new red, raised line. Yet more accidents occurred and scars accumulated until my mom warned me not to ever hurt myself again: she was too tired to make another sixty-mile trip to the emergency room.

Now when I visited my grandma, she smeared beef suet on the restitched parts of my face and there was an unspoken message that I could no longer bank on my beauty getting me anywhere. Since my parents thought I was fine, she took it upon herself to explain the cold, hard facts to me: beyond my scars, my hair was a mess, my unmanicured fingernails a scandal, and my table manners terrible. I tried to sink below her critical radar by spending hours hiding behind her couch—further evidence to her of my lack of proper spirit.

By second grade I still couldn't read with any fluency, and even my mother, who worked as a school music teacher, admitted that my progress on the piano lessons was the worst she had ever witnessed. I was also going through a sickly phase. For most kids, illness was treated with rest, saltine crackers, soda, and heavy doses of television. Because our valley was beyond the reach of TV waves, I spent my childhood sick-days listening to my mom read to me, or crafting potholders on a little red potholder loom. Every time another round of strep throat or flu took me down, I spent hours stretching knitted loops across that frame. The satisfying feeling of weaving loops under-over, under-over was followed by the rather tense thrill of popping off the loops and lacing them through each other as they shrank back to their former size, holding each other in a woven grip. I experimented and found that arranging and weaving the loops in different orders made checks or stripes, and certain color combinations created different moods. A long illness meant my mom or dad had to make an hour trip into town for more aspirin, Jell-O, and a new supply of those colored loops for my loom. It also meant that the drawer next to the stove was stuffed with a kaleidoscopic collection of potholders.

I had finally found my calling: I was a bona fide potholder prodigy.

- - - -

Of course, any household needs only a few potholders. They are, after all, really only good for holding hot pots; never can they disguise themselves as scarves, belts, or hats. Thus, all our relatives received potholders as presents—more than they too would ever need.

So it was that my grandmother discovered my one true talent. My output was considered prodigious for someone so lacking in other apparent skills. I was, she proclaimed, "Good With My Hands," and something had to be done about it. "You should learn to do something with them," she would say to me, "I don't want you to end up pushing the pencil for someone else." She spoke to me as if my hands were my vocation, literally calling me to my destiny: "Do something with me! Anything!" After failing at nearly everything else, how could I ignore something I was good at?

Yet my grandmother didn't have the time or inclination to instruct me in feminine handwork; she was too busy practicing her sharpshooting skills on animals that unsuspectingly trespassed upon her domain. My mother was overworked running a ranch house, cooking massive meals in a frying pan two feet across, teaching music, and selling imported harpsichords. My other grandmum, the one my brother called "the really *nice* one," lived far away and hadn't been able to impart knitting to my fingers. So, my grandmother found a surrogate grandma who would instruct my nimble fingers in crochet.

Who knew, maybe I would become an idiot savant with a hook?

Mrs. Samplee was an elderly southern lady who was also Good With Her Hands. She summered in a nearby village of rock-hounds with her retired Methodist minister husband. Like others in this colony, they had a little cottage just big enough for their minimal needs, a garage where they held potluck parties, and a big pile of ore from the nearby sapphire mine that they picked through while sitting outside in lawn chairs. I remember Mrs. Samplee as a slight, fair lady with crinkly eyes that actually sparkled. I would stare intently—maybe even rudely—at her, not wanting to miss a beam of light that sometimes spangled out of her blue eyes.

Our first crochet lesson was quite successful. I mastered yarn tension and the hook hold, and I managed to make a chain. Like the simple rhythm of weaving under-over, under-over, I enjoyed the feeling of hooking yarn and twisting it through a loop. And then another loop. And another.

It was so easy that I went home and churned out yards and yards of crochet chain in the ghastly variegated tones available only in 1970s discount yarn brands. I made chains so that, come winter, everyone's mittens could be connected together through their coat sleeves. Then I made more chains. The crochet chains flowed from my hook just as potholders had popped off my loom.

Except that even potholders were a bit more useful.

Pleased with my virtuosity, Mrs. Samplee decided we could move right on to granny squares. Now, however, I had to do more than let my hands go on auto-pilot. I had to concentrate on learning a series of moves in a certain order. The foundation ring of chain 6 was no problem, and row 2 went well, as I just had to repeat *double crochet three times, chain three* until I made a round. But, by the time I got to the third row, the twinkling eyes and ticking clock would start to distract me. I remember needing reminders on where to start, and then forgetting when to do what. Mrs. Samplee tried to explain to me how I could know what stitch to do in which place. Then, she would gently have to remind me of the order of stitches.

My problem was that I thought the secret to making a granny square was to memorize the series of double crochets and chains that altered slightly on each of five rows. I

- - - -

felt that mastering the granny square was like learning to perform a complicated series of dance steps without music to lead the feet, or completing secret maneuvers that could never be committed to writing lest they fall into the hands of the enemy. I didn't trust myself to try and figure it out and I didn't know that ripping out mistakes and trying a new tack is part of the learning process. I did know that as soon as I got home the memory of the exact order of stitches started to fade until I was back to making more chains.

The next week I would show up at Mrs. Samplee's for what started to feel like remedial tutoring, learning how to make a granny square all over again. I was able to make some squares under tutelage, but I started to feel that although I was still Good With My Hands, I wasn't so good with remembering what to do with them.

After several weeks of dealing with my short-term memory loss, Mrs. Samplee asked me if I was enjoying myself. I admitted that crochet was okay, but not as satisfying as making potholders. In fact, I think we both knew that every time I had to be reintroduced to the granny square, my self-esteem unraveled another link. Years of directing recreational activities for church groups made my would-be mentor a kind and resourceful lady, and before saying goodbye at my last lesson, she gave my father and I the address of a sock factory down south that might send me some free loops to keep me on my potholder path. My dad mailed off a request for some loops and, true to form, I forgot all about it.

Fall arrived, I entered third grade, the Samplees moved back to Florida for the winter, and a new family of ten boys moved in down the road. After years of being the only child my age within eight miles, I ran wild with someone my own age instead of tagging along behind my big brothers. I also learned to read in an explosion, jumping a few grade levels in a few months. Instead of stumbling through flat narratives about Jimmy, Sue, and their dog Pepper, I whizzed through fantastical stories about giant peaches and orphaned girls who were actually princesses. In fact, I was so busy playing and reading, I forgot I was scarred, unmanicured, and Good With My Hands. By the time flu season arrived that year, I no longer needed to burn through bags of loops or make yards of crochet chains to divert myself.

The next spring, we got a call from the local Burlington Northern freight house. They had a large crate for us sent from North Carolina; if we paid the substantial C.O.D. shipping charges, we could pick it up. My family spent days speculating on what the mysterious package could be. My mother wasn't expecting any harpsichords nor had my father won any bids on army-surplus equipment lately. The next time we went to town, we stopped by the freight office and asked if we could just look at the box—maybe that would help us remember what we had ordered. The cardboard box was about a yard square and sat on a wooden pallet, so there were a lot of things we *imagined* it could hold. Finally, Dad paid the shipping costs and the box was loaded by forklift into the back of our pick-up truck. We got in the truck bed and cut the box open. Sock loops. Thousands, maybe millions, of sock loops. And they were *all* white.

It was enough to kill any remaining interest I had in the fiber arts.

My grandmother died long ago now, and I stopped being afraid of her a few years after that. Turns out she was wrong about some things. For one thing, I'm not that stupid after all and nobody cares much about the state of my fingernails. But she was right about some other things. It's true, you can't bank on beauty. And, yes, beef suet must be good for the skin; my face is just fine.

For years I avoided both potholders and crochet. To be honest, I wasn't inspired by the crochet creations I saw. Plastic bread-bags hooked into welcome mats, long meshy vests in vivid orange, or Budweiser beer-can panels with holes punched around the edges crocheted together into hats—these things held no fascination for me.

In the intervening years, my mom taught me how to sew and—with some help from a friend—I learned to knit. I wasn't a natural at knitting. Squarish garter-stitch garments were easy for my hands to master. Projects involving trickier techniques like purling, increasing, and decreasing sometimes reduced me to tears, or, more commonly, fits involving unladylike language. But I knew enough to avoid crochet. Once I made it through the tears and swearing stage, I became proficient, and then obsessed. I'm still waiting to become masterful.

Then, last summer, I picked up a crochet hook again. My older son was sick and bored, desperatcly bored. First, I thought I would try and teach him the relaxing and useful craft of knitting. True to family tradition, the knitting needles ended up across the room, seemingly propelled there by foul language. Then I remembered that as a child I too had been completely unable to manage knitting, but was at

– – – –

least able to crochet a chain. I always carry some crochet hooks in my knitting bag to fix dropped stitches, and have more yarn stock than some stores, so tools and raw material were not a problem. My fingers found their old groove too—all those hours churning out chain stitch were not for nothing. I showed my son how to hold the hook and yarn and make a stitch. Sure enough—the boy is mine—he quickly made a yard of chain.

It all felt sort of familiar, a quiet, sort of boring summer day spent relearning how to hold yarn and hook, to make a chain. Knowing we had to avoid the granny square, I looked in my *Big, Big Book of Needlecraft* and decided he could try to make a hat in single crochet. When the going got slow for him, I offered to do "just a few rows." And as I grew tired of watching the chart for my two-color knitting project, I begged him to let me do "just a few more rows." Thus it was that thirty years after learning crochet, I finally finished (with help from my son) a crocheted garment. We even fought over who got to wear it.

Meanwhile, as I was hogging the crochet project, the anti-potholder spell was broken. Just a few weeks earlier, I had felt compelled to buy a couple bags of deeply, vividly colorful loops during Crazy Days at a small town variety store. Of course, I still have a little red metal potholder loom. One night I pulled the loops and loom out of my closet and left them in the kitchen thinking the next day I might show my son what I had once found so compelling. Next morning, stumbling into the kitchen, I tripped over the loom—with a potholder already stretched across the pegs.

"Mama, while I start your tea, could you please finish the edges off so I can make another one?" my son begged. Now we have a full drawer of colorful potholders next to our stove—and presents at the ready for the relatives.

With the potholder spell broken, it was time to break another curse. I rummaged around for some rough wool in inspiring earthy colors. (I didn't want to be confused by any variegated acrylic flashbacks to my youth.) Then, I got out that *Big, Big Book of Needlework* again and opened it right up to the page entitled "Anyone Can Do the Granny Square!" My heart sank when I saw the directions were written in what appeared to be some secret granny code consisting solely of abbreviations strung between asterisks and parenthesis.

Then I remembered: I have a granny square afghan I had "rescued" from a thrift shop. Soon I held in my lap the written directions *and* the afghan so that both were in view, and I chained on. With the hook and yarn in my hands, and my visual aids, it became obvious. There is a simple— very simple—granny-logic that makes a granny square grow. When I studied what my hands were working on and visualized where I wanted to go, the answer was right there, under my fingers, its own little granny textile engineering revealing itself, urging me on. "Come on," my incipient square urged, "you *are* Good With Your Hands!"

So I guess my grandmother was right about another thing. To prove it, I finished off a perfect granny square.